Sir William Muir

The Beacon of Truth

Testimony of the Coran to the truth of the Christian religion

Sir William Muir

The Beacon of Truth
Testimony of the Coran to the truth of the Christian religion

ISBN/EAN: 9783337262396

Printed in Europe, USA, Canada, Australia, Japan

Cover: Foto ©Lupo / pixelio.de

More available books at **www.hansebooks.com**

THE BEACON OF TRUTH

MORRISON AND GIBB, PRINTERS EDINBURGH.

OR

TESTIMONY OF THE CORAN

TO THE

TRUTH OF THE CHRISTIAN RELIGION

Translated from the Arabic

BY SIR WILLIAM MUIR, K.C.S.I.,
LL.D., D.C.L., PH.D.

"*Buy the truth, and sell it not.*"—PROV. xxiii. 23

LONDON

THE RELIGIOUS TRACT SOCIETY

56 PATERNOSTER ROW AND 65 ST. PAUL'S CHURCHYARD

1894

CONTENTS

	PAGE
INTRODUCTION BY THE TRANSLATOR .	7
PREFACE	11

CHAPTER I

Passages of the Coran to the effect that Mohammed was not "sent" with signs or miracles, and that in point of fact he showed none 13

CHAPTER II

Passages of the Coran signifying that Mohammed was not sent to use force or compel men to join his religion . 33

CHAPTER III

Passages of the Coran that cancel, and passages that are cancelled 55

CHAPTER IV

Passages of the Coran testifying that the Tourât and the Gospel have not been altered, nor suffered verbal corruption 78

CHAPTER V

Passages of the Coran showing that Prophecy and Revelation belong to the Beni Israel . . . 104

CHAPTER VI

Passages of the Coran pointing to the Divinity of the Lord Jesus Christ 122

CONCLUSION 150

INTRODUCTION BY THE TRANSLATOR

THE *Minâr ul Hakk* is a treatise designed to show the evidence in support of Christianity contained in the Coran,—a *Beacon*, as it were, pointing to the faith of the Gospel. Purely apologetic, the translation is hardly suited, like that of the *Sweet First-Fruits*, for English use. To the ordinary reader, indeed, unfamiliar with the tenets and dialectics of Islam, the course of the argument—however powerful and convincing to a follower of the Arabian Prophet—will appear strange; if not, at times, altogether unintelligible. Still, even for the Western student, the controversy will not be devoid of interest, exhibiting as it does the style of dogmatic reasoning and thought prevalent among Theologians of the East; and the reader may be reminded, here and there, of the memorable colloquies held by Henry Martyn with the Moulvies of Shiraz and Ispahan on his journey to his resting-place at Tokat.

The basis of the argument is the Coran, taken

verse by verse, with the commentaries thereon. First appears the text, then follow the explanations given of it by the Moslem expositors, and lastly, the remarks of the author on what has preceded. Each chapter closes with a review summing up the most important conclusions. The Commentators chiefly relied on are Bokhâri (*d.* 256 A.H.) and the Imâm Fakhr ud Deen Râzi (*d.* 606 A.D.),—authorities much esteemed by orthodox Moslems.

The opening chapters discuss the prophetic claim of Mohammed. In the First, it is proved from an abundance of passages that he showed no miracle, and that the Coran, which is called by his followers a miracle, has, notwithstanding its wonderful beauty and power, no trace of the miraculous about it. In the Second chapter are quoted an array of texts, belonging to the early years of the Prophet's ministry, in which toleration is enjoined and constraint forbidden in matters of religion,—his mission being limited strictly to that of a "Preacher" and "Warner"; —all in irreconcilable contrast with the intolerance and force of later days. The Third chapter is devoted to the question of "Cancelment," that is, of texts and commands which, cancelling other texts and commands, take thus their place. Such changes were made in accordance with the expediency of the day, or with the personal desires of Mohammed; and, as such, are shown to be incompatible with the assumption that their source is divine.

The second half of the volume takes up the evidences of the Christian faith as derived from the Coran.

Chapter Four contains texts which prove that the Tourât and the Gospel are authentic and genuine, and their teaching obligatory on the professor of Islam. The Fifth chapter proves, in a similar way, that the gift of prophecy and revelation runs by divine promise in the line of Israel alone; while the Sixth is reserved for texts which contain clear admission of the divine nature of Jesus the Messiah. The Concluding chapter sums up the whole argument, and leaves the lesson with the fair and intelligent Moslem, that the follower of the Coran is bound to believe in the Old and New Testaments, and there to find for himself the way of life which is but dimly shadowed forth in his own faith. The Coran leads the inquirer, as it were, to the portal of Christianity, and there stops short. The *Beacon of Truth* invites him to mark the finger which nevertheless points to the Scriptures, to enter in, and there be guided to the faith in Jesus, the Saviour of the world.

The work from beginning to end is an *argumentum ad hominem*, from the conclusions of which it seems impossible for the believer in the Coran to escape. It is drawn with admirable power, and close familiarity with Moslem sentiment and dogma. It is also written in language of singular grace and beauty, vigorous throughout and often impassioned. The discussion, though searching, is conducted with as much amenity and forbearance as the tenacious and conclusive character of the reasoning admitted. In fine, without claiming that the treatise is in all its parts equally powerful, or that the arguments here and there may not to some appear defective or weak, I am unhesitatingly of opinion that, taken as a whole, no apology of the Christian faith carrying similar weight and cogency has ever been addressed to the Mahometan world. And I look upon it as the duty of the Church—should this opinion be concurred in—to take measures for the translation of the *Minâr ul Hakk* into the vernacular of every land inhabited by those professing the Moslem faith, and to see that all Missionaries in these lands have the means of becoming familiar with its contents.

W. M.

EDINBURGH, 1894.

PREFACE

PRAISE be to the LORD who hath revealed the BOOK, "a Light and a Guide to men of understanding"; and hath, by manifest evidence, established the same as a Message from Heaven, for every age to the end of time.

Now, seeing that Moslems have in their Coran the most excellent testimony to the purity, authenticity, and authority of the Tourât and the Gospel, and also a light illustrating the Divinity of the Messiah;—

Seeing also that most part of them in the present day, accuse the Scriptures of having been changed and corrupted; and further, that they look upon the Messiah as but one of the great Prophets,—albeit amongst the Chiefest;—as if they had read only parts of the Coran, and never studied the many verses which clearly prove the genuineness of the Scriptures, and give the MESSIAH a place beyond all others,—the place of the WONDERFUL;—

Seeing all this, I was burdened in spirit, and humbly prayed to the Almighty that HE would show to them the truth respecting His Son by means of their own writings. Musing thus on the best way for this end, I was in God's providence led to study the various works which, after the Coran, are held by the Moslems to carry greatest weight in religious matters,—such as the *Sunnat*, or Custom of the Prophet; the *Sîrat*, or Biography of the Prophet; the *Ahiya i Alûm* of Imâm Ghazâli; the Commentaries on the Coran by the Imâm Al Fakhr Al Râzi, by the Imâm Al Beidhâwi, and by Jelâlein. These I carefully perused, and extracted what was most important in them. Then, to the best of my ability, I sought out passages from the Coran itself, bearing on the truth of the Christian faith, with the interpretations given of them by these several authorities. And when, with God's help, the required materials had been thus got together, I arranged them as they appear in this treatise, with my own observations, a review at the close of each chapter, and an address which sums up the whole.

A small and unpretending book, this aims with the help of the Almighty at a great blessing,—attracting him whom, without the divine help, there is no hope of attracting; so that as he stands by the spring he may quench his thirst thereat. Well aware of my want of skill in the art of writing, I fear that there may be faults and deficiencies in my work; and I therefore look to the gentle reader to excuse whatever he may find of weakness and imperfection, and to correct any error or oversight, as it becometh the generous to do.

Fare ye well!

THE BEACON OF TRUTH

CHAPTER I

PASSAGES OF THE CORAN TO THE EFFECT THAT MOHAMMED WAS NOT "SENT" WITH SIGNS OR MIRACLES, AND THAT IN POINT OF FACT HE SHOWED NONE

1. *They say, "Why hath not a sign been sent down unto him from his Lord?" SAY, "Verily God is able to send down a sign, but the greater part of them do not understand."*—SURA AL INÂM (vi.) v. 37.

Commentary.—Râzi observes that the objection in the text is one of those raised against the Prophet by the Unbelievers, namely, that if he had been sent of God, his mission would have been attested by miracles. Why, then, did Mohammed reply that God was able to send miracles? The answer indicates that the Coran was intended as a miracle which could not be gainsaid; and as the Unbelievers were not able in this to contradict the Prophet, it shows that the Coran really was a miracle. How then are we to explain the repeated objection made by the Unbelievers, "Why hath no sign been sent down unto him from his Lord"?

The Imâm in reply gives alternative answers

First, The people may have objected that the Coran belonged to the class of writings, like the Tourât, the Psalms, and the Gospel, which did not profess to be miracles, and because of this doubt they still called for a miracle.

Second, Or the miracles called for may have been of the kind shown by the prophets of old, as dividing the sea, uplifting the hills, or raising the dead. To this it is replied, that "God is able to send down a miracle," that is, of the kind demanded, but that "most of them do not understand"; which means, according to the Sunnat, that the Coran is a clear and infallible miracle, and that, being so, it were vain and impious to demand more of the Lord, with whom it rests to give such or to withhold; or, according to the Motazelites, other miracles were withheld because not expedient.

Third, Or the reason may have been that a clear miracle already given had left the Unbelievers no excuse. Supposing God to have granted their unreasonable demand, they might have gone on calling for a second, a third, and a fourth sign, and so on, without end, in which event proof and objection would have had no finality. It was necessary, therefore, to shut the door, and let the miracle (of the Coran) already granted suffice.

Fourth, or lastly, Had God granted the kind of miracles they called for, and yet after all they had continued in unbelief, they would, like those of old, have made themselves liable to destruction; and so it was in mercy, though they knew it not, that the Lord, by withholding what they asked for, saved them from that doom.—*Râzi.*

So *Beidhawi*: "The greater part do not understand," that is, what they are asking for. God, it is true, was able to send down the kind of miracles demanded; but had their desire been granted, they would have exposed themselves, continuing in unbelief, to calamity, while the miracle already given (in the Coran) was of itself sufficient without it.

Remarks.—Surely the Coreish were not to be blamed because they demanded of Mohammed a sign like to the signs shown by the prophets of old. The answer, that "God is able to give them a sign," was no answer at all, and justified the reply, "True, God is able to give signs; for, to show forth His power, He gave signs to the prophets of old, as Moses and Jesus; and if Mohammed be as one of them, let him show us like signs, that we may believe."

Again, had the people recognised the Coran to be a miracle, it would have satisfied them; and if so, why this reply, that "God was able to send down a miracle," and not rather, "Here is the Coran, take that, for it is a miracle"? But here rejoinder by the Prophet's opponents would have been easy, for the Arabs were well acquainted with the wonderful compositions of their poets and orators, as Imrul Cays, Nábigha, Coss, etc.; and though no one could equal the beauty of their works, they were never regarded as miracles. And if the Coran had really been a miracle, like raising of the dead, dividing of the sea, etc., then why should Mohammed not also have shown other miracles like these; and how would that have cast any reflection on the wisdom of God?

Similarly, to say that had their request been granted they might have asked for a second, third, and fourth miracle, is mere conjecture. It might equally be asserted, that they would have been satisfied with a single real miracle. Their demand was simply as if they had said, "How can we accept Mohammed's claim to be a prophet, when he fails to show a single miracle in proof of his mission, as did the prophets of old? let him show one, and we will believe." Equally fallacious is it to say that this would have been an unreasonable and impious demand; on the contrary, it was all the more reasonable, seeing that the Prophet came with a new faith differing from that of the Beni Israel and the Christians, and the religion of the country; and their refusal to accept this new religion without some miracle like those of the old prophets, is rather a proof of their sagacity and sincerity than of unreasonable obstinacy.

11. *And when thou dost not show unto them a sign, they say,* " *Why hast thou avoided to bring it?* " Say, "*Verily, I follow that only wherewith the Lord hath inspired me.*" *This (revelation) is a witness from your Lord,—a guide and a mercy to the people that believe.—* Sura Al Arâf (vii.) v. 204.

Commentary.—The Arabs demanded from Mohammed a sign from heaven in proof of his mission; to which he replied, that failure to show a miracle, as they demanded of him, was a groundless accusation, seeing that the Coran itself was a clear and infallible miracle—one sufficient to prove his mission; and that such being the case, the call for anything further was an unwarrantable and profane demand.—*Râzi.*

Remarks.—Apparently the Arabs in all sincerity asked Mohammed for a sign in proof of his ministry, not recognising the Coran as such. Thus, among themselves, they would say, " If he would only show us a real miracle"; and when they met him, "Why dost thou avoid it? Show us a sign like those of the prophets of old, else we will not accept thee." His answer was that he only followed that which was revealed to him by his Lord. Was this any reply to those who asked for a sign to prove his ministry? Never!

111. *The Unbelievers say,* " *Why hath not a sign been given him by his Lord? Nay, but thou art only a*

Warner; and unto every people there hath been given a guide."—SURA AL RÁD (xiii.) v. 8.

Commentary.—Mohammed was sent as a Warner, just as a guide and preacher had been sent to every people before him. So also as to miracles. God puts all in this respect upon an equality, suiting the kind of miracle to the special circumstances of each people. Thus, magic or sorcery being in the ascendant in the days of Moses, the miracles shown by him were of that nature; and the healing art being practised in the time of Jesus, it was suitable that his miracles should be such as raising the dead, curing the leper and the blind, etc. For the same reason, as beauty of composition was the distinguishing feature of the Prophet's time, the miracle given to him was the wondrous eloquence of the Coran; and so, if the Arabs would not believe, notwithstanding that this miracle was specially designed for them, it is clear that they would not have been convinced by any other kind of miracle. "Thou art but a Warner"; that is, "Thy duty is simply to preach: to guide men into the right way belongs to God alone."—*Rázi.*

And *Beidhawi*: When his people demanded such miracles as those of Moses and Jesus, Mohammed is told that he was only a preacher like those before him. He had no concern with the signs they called for; he was but a guide to point out the right way. God alone was able to answer the demand, and it was withheld because made perversely, and not with a sincere desire for conviction.

Remarks.—The reader will observe that Rázi's comment is not apposite to the text, which contains no hint of the Coran being a miracle, but simply states that the Prophet being nothing more than a Warner, his duty is only to preach. The rest of his words are equally wide of the mark. For, *first,* some of Moses' signs had nothing to do with magic, as the death of the Egyptians' first-born, the destruction of Pharaoh's army, and the issuing of water from the rock. And so also many of Jesus' miracles had no reference to the healing art,—as the creation of a bird from clay, and descent of the table from heaven, according to the Coran; or the feeding of multitudes from a few loaves, and walking on the water, according to the Gospel. Moreover, other prophets, as Joshua, Elias, Elisha, and the apostles, showed various miracles similar to those of Moses and Jesus. *Second;* again, the Arabs had no such special claim to eloquence and literary power that their miracle should lie in that direction. Every nation has its own form of eloquence, suited to its taste and language; take, for example, the models of the Jews and Greeks, as is manifest from their wonderful writings in our hands. And if there was neither magic nor the art of healing amongst the Arabs, they certainly were not wanting in intelligence and quick apprehension, and as such equally entitled with the Egyptians and Israelites to expect miracles, and equally qualified to judge of them.

Indeed, as the mission of Moses and of Jesus was established by miracles, it was *à fortiori* incumbent on Mohammed, who sought to introduce a religion differing from theirs and cancelling its obligations, to prove his claim by miracles superior even to theirs, and more wonderful. How, then, are those to be blamed who, when he failed to show such, refused to admit his claim or believe in his mission?

IV. *And nothing hindered Us from sending (thee) with miracles, but that those of old time gave them the lie.*—SURA BENI ISRAEL (xvii.) v. 58.

Commentary.—We are told that people came to Mohammed saying that the prophets of old showed miracles, such as causing the winds to blow, and raising the dead, etc. "Now show us," said they, "some miracle like these, and we shall believe." The reply here signifies that were such miracles shown to them, and they still continued in infidelity, they would have become liable, like the nations of old, to the doom of extermination. It was thus in goodness and mercy that the Lord withheld their request, knowing that some of them would eventually believe, or would have believing progeny.—*Rázi.*

Beidhawi gives a similar explanation, instancing the tribes of Ad and Thamud, which, on rejecting the miracles which they called for, were swept away.

Remarks.—It does not appear where the Commentators got this notion of people being destroyed for rejecting miracles. The Egyptians were not exterminated; some were destroyed, but only some. So with the Beni Israel; many a time they denied their prophets, yet they were never swept away, but remained a people, as they are at this day. It is the same with the tale of the Adites and Thamudites; even supposing that (like the Tusam and Judeis) they did disappear, it may have been because of their abounding iniquity or internecine warfare. The rise and fall of nations is the natural law of God. It is His to create and His to destroy, with a purpose beyond our finite wisdom.

Again, we know of no people to whom a prophet was sent (as were Moses and Jesus) with miracles, but some of them believed. Now, seeing that Mohammed came without a miracle, and yet very soon a great number of the Coreish accepted his mission, and not long after the whole city of Yathreb also, would it possibly have been otherwise even if the Lord had sent Mohammed with miracles like those of the prophets of old? If his people accepted him without a miracle, what ground is there for the comment that "no miracle was given him lest, having belied it, they should have incurred the doom of extermination"? They received him without a miracle; why should they have rejected him if he had shown one? So the interpretation of the Commentators falls utterly to pieces. If, indeed, after all his warnings, the people had still rejected Mohammed because he failed to show miracles like those of Moses and Jesus, then indeed there might have been some sort of ground for saying that they would not have believed, even after witnessing miracles. But this was not the case, for we know that Khadija accepted her husband as a prophet at the very opening of his mission, and, shortly after, his cousin Aly, Abu Bekr, Othman, and Omar; and in the course of a few years the whole of Mecca, even those who had demanded miracles as the condition of believing on him. Now, all this was known to the Almighty beforehand; how then can it be said (as we are told is the meaning of the text) that God withheld miracles, knowing that, if granted, the Coreish would belie them, as did the nations of old? Shall words be attributed to the Most High inconsistent thus with His foreknowledge? God forbid!

V. *They say, "Why hath not a sign been sent down unto him from his Lord?"* SAY, *"Signs belong unto the Lord: as for me, I am but a plain preacher."*— SURA AL ANKÁBÛT (xxix.) v. 48.

ON ABSENCE OF MIRACLES 21

Commentary.—The people thus addressed the Prophet, "Thou sayest that a Book hath been sent down unto thee, like to that sent down unto Moses and Jesus. But it is not so, for Moses showed nine miracles to prove the heavenly origin of his Book; and no sign hath been sent down unto thee." In reply, God instructed Mohammed to say, "Signs come from the Lord alone, and are not a condition of the prophetic office. I am but a prophet: it rests with the Lord, if He will, to show a miracle; or, if He will, to withhold the same. As for me, I have no concern with miracles. I am simply a Warner, with no power beyond."—*Râzi.*

Beidhawi and Jelalein have similar remarks, the latter adding, "Sâlih showed the miracle of the camel, Moses of the rod, and Jesus of the table; as for me (said the Prophet), I am but a plain preacher, warning the wicked of hell-fire."

Remarks.—On this and the preceding passages, one may remark how natural it was for those about him to ask Mohammed for signs in proof of his mission, such as Moses and Jesus showed. That "miracles were in God's hand" was no sufficient answer; and it is evident that they did not regard the Coran as a miracle, or they would have been satisfied with it as such. Again, the text shows, that instead of coming with signs, Mohammed professed to be simply a preacher, warning the people of future punishment; an excellent office done by others as well as by apostles and prophets, out of love for their people's welfare. Miracles are said not to be a necessary condition of a divine mission. True; there have been prophets, like Jeremiah and Jonah, sent of God without signs. But no prophet, *commissioned to deliver a law,* came unsupported by miracles and signs; and Mohammed set himself not only to deliver a law, but to cancel an existing dispensation founded upon miracles. It was therefore all the more incumbent on him (as we have said before) to have supported his claim by miracles, even greater and more numerous than those of the former lawgivers.

VI. *What? Doth it not suffice them that I have sent down unto thee the Book which is recited unto them?*—SURA AL ANKÁBÛT (xxix.) v. 49.

Commentary.—The meaning is, that if miracles be a necessary condition, one hath already appeared, namely, the Coran, which is a manifest and continuing miracle. " Doth it not suffice to them ? "—meaning that this revelation is a more perfect miracle than others that have preceded it.—*Râzi.*

And *Beidhawi*: The Coran is a miracle, better than any they have demanded ; for its perusal is a continuing sign that shall not pass away, but shall remain with them for ever. And so also *Jelalein.*

Remarks.—In this text, again, there is nothing implying (as the Commentators say) that the Coran is a miracle. So far from its appearing as a miracle, the people did not even accept it as a revelation, for they said, " Surely this is a story which he hath fabricated with the aid of strangers " (S. Al Forcán (xxiv.) v. 4). Many amongst the Moslems themselves question its being a miracle. Take, for example, the arguments both for and against its miraculous character, as given in the *Kitâb al Muâfic:*—

1. *The Coran held to be a miracle.*—It is so held because it is impossible to produce the like (اعجازه). It challenges comparison by its beauty, being superior to anything that ever appeared in

Arabia. Some, however, believe the language itself not to be beyond rivalry, apart from the truth conveyed, the like of which it would be impossible to produce.

Others hold the miraculous to consist in the revelation of the unknown, as in the prophecy, "The Greeks, after their discomfiture, shall shortly defeat the Persians in a few years"; the word "few" (بضع) signifying from three to nine: and so it came to pass.

Some, again, believe the miracle to lie in the absence of discrepancies in the Coran, notwithstanding its length, quoting the divine words, "If it had been from any other than God, they would surely have found many discrepancies therein."

Another view is that the miracle consists in "prevention" (الصرف), which signifies that imitation was rendered impossible by divine hindrance; that is to say, the Arabs, though aforetime able to produce a work equal to the Coran, were unable by supernatural prevention to do so afterwards. According to the Motazelites,[1] the miracle consists in the Almighty "turning men aside" from the attempt, though they otherwise possessed the power. A Shie-ite writer (Murtaza) holds the "prevention" to consist in God's "taking away the knowledge" necessary for successful imitation, and so it became impossible.

II. *The Coran held* (by certain of the Moslems themselves) *to be not a miracle.*—*First*, The proof of the miraculous must be so evident as to admit of no doubt. And the variety of opinion as to what constitutes the Coran a miracle is so great as to make it inadmissible. *Second*, The several proofs are in themselves insufficient.

First, As to the beauty of the Coran. When we look, say the objectors, at the works of our great orators and poets, and compare them, say, with the shorter Suras (for the challenge, "produce a Sura the like thereof," applies equally to them), we find no superior beauty; nay, often the balance inclines the other way: whereas in a miracle there must be no room for doubt; the evidence must be absolute.

Second, The Companions doubted certain pieces being part of the Coran; for example, Ibn Masûd held the Fâtcha and the Incantatory Suras (the last two), though the best known in the

---

[1] The Motazelites (supported by the Caliph Al Mamun and his two successors) deny the Coran to be eternal and uncreate.

whole Coran, not to belong to it. Now, if the style had reached the point required to prove it a miracle, that same style must have sufficed to distinguish what was the Coran from what was not, and they had not differed about it.

Third, While the Coran was being collected, if a verse or a couple of verses were presented by some one not known to the collectors, these were not entered in the collection excepting on oath and evidence of the occasion on which revealed, etc. Now, had the diction itself been evidence of the miraculous, the collectors would have recognised it thereby, and have had no need of further evidence.

Fourth, We find in compositions throughout the world various degrees of excellence, without any fixed limit being reached impossible to surpass; and so in every age there must be someone who has excelled his compeers, even if in time to come there should arise someone surpassing him again. Now, supposing Mohammed to have been the most eloquent of his age; if that is to be proof of a miracle, it follows that the work of any man which surpasses those of all others of his time is a miracle,—a manifest absurdity!

Passing on to the evidence of the miraculous, arising from the absence of discrepancies, notwithstanding the length of the Coran, the arguments are as follows. First, it is objected that the Coran does contain assertions contrary to fact, as in the verse, "We have not omitted from the Book any single thing"; and, again, "There is nothing in nature, moist or dry, but it is to be found in the manifest Book." This is not the case, for we find no mention whatever in the Coran of many matters, the healing art, the daily phenomena of nature, and so forth; so that the statements in such texts are not in accord with fact.

Next, there are discrepancies in such expressions as in هذان لساحران; and when certain pages of the Coran were put before Othman, he said, "Verily, herein are slips which will catch the Arab tongue." Then there is much useless tautology, as in Sura Al Rahman; and repetition over and over of histories, as those of Moses and Jesus; and such superflous words as in تلك عشرة كاملة. And, after all, what defect is greater than useless verbiage?

Again we read, "Had it (the Coran) been from any other than God, they would have found many discrepancies therein,"—signifying that the absence of discrepancies is proof of a writing being divine. Now, on the contrary, says this writer, there are throughout the Coran numerous faults and discrepancies, verbal and idiomatic, as well as in the sense.[1]

And as to discrepancies, in many of our most beautiful poems and writings we find no defects of any kind, not to say discrepancies. Now, taking a short Sura (for the challenge applies equally to them), are we to say that the absence of contradiction in that amount of prose or poetry is proof of its being a miracle? And yet this is the line of reasoning!

Lastly, as to the argument from "prevention";—the miracle would consist in the prevention, not in the Coran. As if one were to say, "I stand up, but ye are unable to rise," and so it came to pass; the miracle would not be in him who stood up, but in the prevention of the others from rising up. And so this illustration is fatal to the old argument that the Coran is a miracle, because others were held back ("prevented") from producing the like.

Rejoinder of those who hold the Coran a miracle.—The variety of opinion as to what that is which proves the Coran a miracle, is not really any ground of weakness. Supposing even the arguments of some of its supporters to be weak, there is absolute unanimity as to the unapproachable beauty and perfection of the Coran as a whole, in its style and rhythm, as well as in its revelation of the unseen, proving it to be a miracle; and the variety of argument complained of is simply due to variety of view and knowledge in the several observers.

Next, the doubts ascribed to some of the Companions as to certain of the Suras being part of the Coran, are mere conjecture, and vanish before the whole collection as handed down to us by a continuous chain. And even if we admitted that the Companions had doubts as to certain parts, we say that they never doubted the Coran as a whole having been revealed to the Prophet, nor its miraculous beauty, but merely as to whether certain parts belonged to it; and that does not affect our argument.

Again, the evidence required when various persons brought the Collectors one or two separate verses, was not as to the authen-

---

[1] Half a page of these is given by the objector, but they are hardly of sufficient importance to quote. They are such as جاءت سكرة: فِي كَالحِجارة instead of ذكانت كالحجارة الموت بالحق instead of الحق بالموت, etc.

ticity of the verses themselves, but as to the place in the Coran they were to occupy in reference to other passages. This was needful, because the revelation came from the mouth of the Prophet from time to time; and evidence was necessary not as to the matter itself, but as to the occasion of its utterance and the place it should appear in. Further, the verbal faults complained of were errors of the scribe, not of the original; as هذان, where the copyist by mistake put in an (ا) for a (ي). The same remark applies to Othman's reference to "slips," which were simply faults of transcription. So also as to surplusage, in the phrase تلك عشرة كاملة the word "complete" was added, though unusual, by way of giving emphasis. The existence of discrepancies, verbal or otherwise, in the successive transcription of copies, is no argument against the Coran being a miracle, but rather the reverse. The only discrepancies that would affect its character would be in the beauty of its composition, and of these there are none.

Lastly, to compare the shorter Suras with lengthy pieces of oratory or poems, is altogether unjust. The comparison is in the eloquence of similar passages, not in those that differ in length, as any fair observer would say. We take our stand on the Coran as a whole, and on the longer Suras, as a proof by their miraculous eloquence of the prophetic mission of Mohammed.

Remarks on the foregoing discussion as to the Coran being a miracle.—We may regard the above argument to be exhaustive, since those who hold the Coran a miracle have here used their best endeavours to extricate themselves from the doubts raised by their co-religionists who question that position. Now, even assuming the Coran to be of consummate eloquence, we see that there is great variety of opinion as to what constitutes it a miracle. Some hold the proof to be simply in the eloquence; others, in its revelation of the Unseen; others, in the absence of discrepancy. Others, again, disagreeing as to the perfect eloquence of the revelation, hold to the doctrine of "prevention," or inability to produce the like, owing to divine intervention. So that there is difference of opinion all round.

Further, it is objected that, to apply the challenge, "Bring a Sura like unto this," to any Sura in the Coran, even the shortest, is unfair. But surely it is not so. For the shorter a piece is, the easier to make it perfect in beauty, and avoid anything weak or defective. Now the argument of the objectors is, that if we take a poem or oration, and compare it even with the shortest of the Suras, we find that the composition of the Arab poets or orators is equal to it, or even superior. The comparison is not with long and short pieces, but with beauty, where even shortness of the Sura gives the Coran the advantage. Where, then, is injustice in the comparison?

To the second objection, that some authorities differ as to the Fâteha and two Incantatory Suras being part of the Coran, it is replied that, even so, there was no difference of view as to the Coran itself being a revelation from God. This is not a satisfactory answer to the argument, that doubts as to certain Suras being part of the Coran weaken the assertion that there was no difference of opinion as to the Coran being a divine revelation. It had been more correct of the defenders to say, "If even we were to admit the doubt, we should still have no difference of opinion as to the rest of the Coran being an inspired revelation," than to say absolutely, "There is no difference of opinion amongst us as to the

Coran being a divine revelation." And so the doubt thus thrown on the Coran as a miracle remains unrebutted.

The answer to the third objection is singularly weak. Tradition tells us that when evidence on oath was required from such as brought separate texts to the Collectors, it was not to prove their being part of the Coran, but simply as to the place they were to be put into. Now, to say of any verse that its place in the Coran was unknown to the Companions, is surely very near to saying that they did not know whether it formed part of the Coran at all. For the Coran professes to be a revelation arranged (like the Scriptures) in parts, chapters, and verses. When, therefore, single verses were produced, if (as is suggested) the position and context of such verses were unknown, the Collectors were bound to take evidence, so as, after a legal fashion, to prove that they formed part of the Coran itself. For we are told that after the Prophet's death, the people brought verses written on pieces of stone, or bone, or palm-leaves, to the Companions collecting the Coran, who, when other proof was wanting, took evidence on oath. Had the Collectors been already satisfied that such texts were parts of the Coran, and been doubtful only of their place in the revelation, we should have heard of their examining the persons bringing them as to the occasion, the time, and the spot on which the witness heard the words from the Prophet's lips; but we read of nothing of the kind in tradition. The presumption therefore remains, as the objectors put it, that the oath taken from those bringing such passages had reference to the authenticity of the texts themselves. This makes the plea urged against the objectors fall to the ground, and leaves the contention, that evidence had to be brought to prove the verses part of the Coran, untouched.

Next, the reply that the "slips" or "faults" spoken of by Othman were errors of transcription is not valid; for, if so, the Caliph would surely have had them corrected, instead of letting them remain in what was believed to be the Word of God. So also as to the expression تلك عشرة كاملة, the advocate explains that the word "complete" is added to dispel doubt, "although it is unusually strong"—as if any such addition were needed; for who but a fool would mistake 9 for 10? And his admission as to the unusual "strength" of the words only adds force to the argument of the objectors.

Then, how strange is it that the advocate not only denies that discrepancies in word and sense are an argument against the miraculous, but rather holds them to be in favour of it! If he means that they prove there has been no change in the text of the Coran since its collection, the Book being a faithful copy of the original, we readily admit the argument. But how can such discrepancies be proof of perfection? If they existed prior to the collection, and at the time of his revision the Caliph did not adventure to correct them, but (like لذن السلم الحران) kept them as before, then the discrepancies must have been in the original. So that their existence is really an argument against perfection, and an answer to the challenge,

"Had it been from any other than God, they would surely have found many discrepancies therein."

Still stranger is the distinction the advocate of the miraculous draws between discrepancies (or variation) in eloquence, and discrepancies in word and sense, holding that the verse just quoted applies to the former only, and not to the latter; in other words, that a fault in the beauty and style of the Coran would alone affect the miracle, and that a discrepancy in the verbiage or sense would not do so. Are we to conclude, then, that the Coran is divine in respect of its eloquence, and human in respect of its verbiage and sense? Can that be the Moslem faith? Is not the truth, rather, that perfect eloquence in any work is no proof that the work is from God, but only that the eloquence is the gift of God? For are not genius, intelligence, memory, and mental power all the gifts of God, so that when we meet with a man of marvellous eloquence and unparalleled oratorical power we say, "Praise be to the Great Giver!"? Do we ever dream that his eloquence is inspired, or that their author is a prophet? So, let the Coran be ever so beautiful and ever so perfect, we say of the author, it is God who gave the talent; and it is all the same whether the book be inspired or not, or whether it surpass all other efforts—as indeed we find in many writings and poems of the Greeks and Arabs.

From the foregoing discussion it appears that the Moslem is in this dilemma. Should he say the Coran is a miracle in respect of its language and sense, he is met (as even the Moslem objector shows) by discrepancies that destroy the assumption. Should he take simple eloquence as the miracle, the claim is shown to be equally untenable. These conclusions are drawn from the doubts and objections, as we have seen, of Believers themselves; and many of the most learned Grammarians hold the same view on arguments that cannot be gainsaid.

REVIEW

From the texts quoted in this chapter, as well as from the Moslem commentaries thereon, it is clear that no claim of having shown miracles was made by the Prophet; and that the absence of miracles to prove his mission like that of the former prophets, is ascribed to divine compassion, lest the Arabs, rejecting such miracles, should (like the similar nations of old) have become liable to destruction; and hence they were not destroyed when they rejected Mohammed, because he came without miracles. Now, since the Coran is by many held to be a miracle, like the dividing of the sea or raising of the dead, or rather to have been an even greater miracle,[1] it would follow, according to this law, that those who heard it and did not believe should equally have suffered that doom. And since no punishment did come, it would follow that the Coran was not a miracle,—a conclusion which accords with the text, "Nothing hindered us from sending thee with miracles, but that the peoples before thee gave them the lie." The difficulty is not

[1] As Râzi, see p. 22.

to be evaded. If we accept the Coran as a miracle, the text breaks down; on the other hand, if we hold it not a miracle, it will satisfy the objection of those who ask why those who rejected the Prophet were not punished, namely, because he showed no miracle. It is difficult to see how the intelligent Moslem can get out of the maze otherwise than by admitting, as this chapter fully proves, that the Coran was not a miracle.

As to the marvellous tales in the Hadith of miracles shown by the Prophet, such as causing water to flow from between his fingers, satisfying multitudes from a little food, etc., they are regarded by all enlightened Moslems as absolutely worthless. Had there been any single miracle of the kind, it would certainly have been mentioned in the Coran, where Mohammed to those who demanded of him a sign repeatedly says that he was sent with none, and gives the reason. And when the Hadith are at variance with the Coran, the honest Believer must reject the Hadith and accept the Coran.

In fine, every intelligent Moslem must see that the Coran is no sufficient miracle, and that they are only driven to set it up as a miracle because they have none other.

CHAPTER II

PASSAGES OF THE CORAN SIGNIFYING THAT MOHAMMED WAS NOT SENT TO USE FORCE OR COMPEL MEN TO JOIN HIS RELIGION

I. *Let there be no compulsion in religion. Verily, the true direction hath been manifestly distinguished from error. Whosoever, therefore, rejecteth idols and believeth in God, he verily hath laid hold of a strong support that cannot be broken. And God both heareth and seeth.*—SURA BACR (ii.) v. 252.

Commentary.—*First,* The Lord hath not made faith to be a matter of compulsion or force. On the contrary, He hath made it a matter of intelligent adoption and free will; for compulsion and force are not allowable in this life, according to the text, "Whosoever so willeth shall believe, and whosoever so willeth shall disbelieve"; and in another Sura, "If thy Lord so willed, every soul on the earth had believed; why, then, shouldst thou seek to compel men to believe?" Compulsion, therefore, and constraint in religion are not lawful, because they would supersede personal endeavour. *Second,* It is compulsion, as when a believer saith to an infidel, Believe, or else I shall slay thee. To such the Lord saith, "Let there be no compulsion in religion." *Third,* Let it not be said to one who embraceth the faith after war, that he hath embraced it under compulsion; for, if after fighting, he agrees thereto, and his profession of the faith is sound, there is no compulsion here.—*Râzi.*

Beidhawi notes that compulsion is really this—forcing a person to an act he does not approve of, by an attack upon him. Again, the divine command is either absolute (*i.e.* in respect both of the heathen and the People of the Book), in which case cancelled by the text, "Fight against the Unbelievers and the hypocrites"; or it applies exclusively to the people of the Book (Jews and Christians). And of these latter there is a tradition that an Ansâr (citizen of Medina) had two sons who became Christians before the mission of the Prophet; so their father laid hands on them, and would not let them go unless they embraced Islam, which, they declining, the father appealed to Mohammed, crying out, "O Prophet of God, shall a part of my very self enter hell-fire, and I looking quietly on?" Thereupon this verse was revealed, and he let them go.

Jelalein refers to the same tradition.

Remarks.—Both Râzi and Beidhawi make here three notable admissions. First, God does not accept conversion, the result of force and compulsion; second, coercion and violence are unlawful, because they supersede personal endeavour; and third, the text is a distinct prohibition, "Thou shalt not compel." Now, as God does not accept faith the result of force and constraint, it follows that force and constraint are opposed to the will of God; and he who resorts to them makes that to be lawful which in point of fact is unlawful. Moreover, the text condemns force, whether practised at the moment, or intended to be resorted to when a fitting opportunity might hereafter occur. The verse is peremptory, "No force in the faith"; the prohibition absolute. It is also of universal application, as we see from Râzi's first two conclusions. But his further remark, as to conversion following upon war, is not reasonable. It assumes that a person under such circumstances embracing Islam, does so by choice; whereas the presumption is that, defeated in battle, humbled and ruined, and having no alternative, he is driven to abandon his former convictions. How can the Commentators speak of there being "no compulsion" when such things are done? Have they forgotten that Jehad and fighting against heathen and People of the Book are according to the command that the faith shall be everywhere Islam alone; for what else does this text mean, "Fight against them till opposition cease, and the faith be wholly God's"? (Sura Baer, v. 188).

II. *It doth not belong unto thee to direct them; it is God that directeth whom He pleaseth. That which ye spend in alms, it is for your own souls; and ye shall not spend anything, but to obtain the favour of God. And what good thing ye give in alms, it shall be repaid unto you, and ye shall not be treated unjustly.*—SURA BACR (ii.) v. 268.

Commentary.—We are told that certain of the Companions having refused an alms to their unbelieving brethren, the question was referred to the Prophet, who, on this verse being revealed, desired them to give the alms. Others say it was the Prophet himself who declined to give alms to Unbelievers till the text was sent down; and its sense is this:—It is not thy place to be guide to those who oppose thee, or to refuse them alms in order that they may embrace the faith: rather give them alms for the Lord's sake, and delay not thy charity until they are converted, for it is said, "Thou shalt not compel men to become believers." Further, the Lord made known unto His prophet that he was sent a bearer of Good, a Warner to call men unto the Lord, a Light to lighten mankind, and manifest the faith unto them; as to guiding them, it was not his concern; it was all the same to him whether they took the right way or refused. Therefore it was not for him to withdraw his help or alms from them. Again, if he sought to gain them over by withholding charity till they believed, their conversion from motives of bribery would be of no avail: the faith required was one of obedience and free choice. *Rázi.*

Beidhawi explains the passage thus: It is no business of thine to guide men; it is simply thy business to advise them aright, to stir them up to what is right, and to deter them from what is evil. So also *Jelalein*, who, referring to the above tradition, gives the meaning thus: "Thou art not responsible for the conversion of men to Islam, but simply for bearing the message: it belongeth to God to lead; and as to what ye give in charity, the merit thereof returns unto your own souls. We are forbidden to give charity with any motive beyond that."

Remarks.—How fair and excellent is the lesson which these doctors of Islam draw from the text! Pause and consider, intelligent reader. If the offering of alms as an inducement to join the faith be unjustifiable, how much more force! If it were thought wrong to give an Unbeliever charity, lest it should have been taken as a bribe, what shall we say of the wars and rapine, the slavery and terror, by which it is held lawful to compel men to enter Islam![1] And yet how strange and inconsistent with this is Râzi's sentiment, that such as go over to Islam when beaten are not to be held as if they had yielded to compulsion! How can he reconcile such view with these two texts? If we are (according to Jelalein) forbidden to offer an alms in the hope of converting the needy, and if that conversion is alone recognisable which is due to free choice, how can this be reconciled with Jehad for the spread of Islam?

III. *Say unto those to whom the Book hath been given, and to the Heathen, Have ye believed? for if*

[1] The Author here refers to the fate of the Beni Coreitza, a Jewish tribe in the neighbourhood of Medina, who were all beheaded after their surrender (some 800 in number), and their women and children sold into slavery, by command of the Prophet.

they have believed, verily they are guided aright; but if they turn their backs, verily unto thee belongeth only the delivering of the message; for God watcheth over His servants.—SURA AL IMRAN, Medina, (iii.) v. 18.

Commentary.—The Prophet's duty is simply to make use of proofs and argument. This is the sole obligation devolving on him; he has no concern as to how the truth is received. It is the Lord that watcheth and giveth effect to His promises and His threats.—*Râzi.*
Beidhawi: If men believe, they benefit their own souls, saving themselves from destruction; if they turn their backs, thy concern is only to deliver the message: their unbelief will not endamage thee, for thou hast delivered it.
Jelalein: Jews, Christians, and Heathen Arabs are here addressed: if they believe, they are guided away from error; if they turn away, it is thine only to carry the message: it is God who seeth, and will reward His servants according to their works.

Remarks.—The Prophet's duty is here distinctly confined to publishing his message, with the evidence and arguments bearing on it. "It is God that watcheth His servants, and visits them according to their works,"—a clear injunction, "thine to preach, ours to take account,"—limiting the office of the Prophet, and prohibiting resort to war, compulsion, or even denunciation. Having delivered his message, no other obligation remained; just as the debtor of one thousand pieces, having paid the thousand, nothing else remains for him to do. Then why did Mohammed, who was "commissioned none otherwise than as a preacher and a warner," not confine himself within the limit thus imposed upon him?

IV. *Thy people have given it (the Coran) the lie.*

Say, "*I am not the keeper over you. For every announcement there is an appointed time, and shortly ye shall know.*"—Sura Al Inâm (vi.) v. 66.

Commentary.—The Prophet is here told that, not being keeper of his people, it was no concern of his to take them to task for giving the lie to his teaching. He was but a warner; it was for God to take account of their actions. According to Ibn Abbas and the Commentators, this text is cancelled by the passages that command fighting for the faith. The Imâm, however, is not of that opinion, for "every announcement hath its appointed time," may refer to punishment in the future life; but it may also refer to the ascendency of the Moslems over the heathen by war, slaughter, and compulsion in the present.—*Râzi.*

Remarks.—This is now the fourth text signifying that Mohammed was not the Guardian of those who rejected him. As to the cancelment of these verses, one party holds that the order for Jehad took their place, and has since remained the only rule of action; in other words, cancels all the texts enjoining freedom of judgment and condemnatory of compulsion. The Imâm, on the other hand, disowns the cancelment, but recognising, at the same time, the command to use the sword, he fails to explain why these texts have been so expressed; why they so explicitly forbid force, and represent in absolute terms the Prophet's duty to be that of a simple warner and bringer of good tidings. Verse after verse not only denies the use of arms, but condemns everything approaching to interference with free choice in religion; suddenly the Revelation changes, and the Prophet is desired to adopt the very measures, as proper and expedient, which had been so strenuously forbidden! Such a course, by my life, would ill become any intelligent creature; how much less can we dare attribute it to the Most High!

V. *Now have evident demonstrations come unto you from your Lord: whoso seeth the same, it is for his own soul; and he that is blind, it is against the same. I am not a Keeper over you.*—SURA AL INÁM (vi.) v. 104.

Commentary.—He that seeth the truth, and believeth, does so for his own benefit; and he that shutteth his eyes, injureth himself: the Lord is Keeper, not the Prophet. He that maketh the choice is benefited by the same, and gaineth the reward; if driven thereto, the merit would be marred. The text bars force. The Commentators give the meaning thus: "My action towards you in respect of the faith is not that of compulsion; I am no Guardian or Master over you;"—which they say was prior to Jehad, for when that was commanded, Mohammed did become the Keeper over them. Some hold that the command to fight abrogates the present text; but that, says Râzi, is far from being the case. Such Commentators are too fond of cancelment, for Doctors of Divinity very properly limit that to the smallest possible extent.—*Râzi.*

Remarks.—Here we have a fifth text to the same effect, in which note three points. (1) Mohammed was in no way responsible for the conduct of Unbelievers, or for any punitive action towards them. (2) Compulsion invalidates merit and recompense. (3) The Lord holds men absolutely free in matters of faith and worship—punishing them if they disobey, and rewarding them if they submit. Now, as to these principles being superseded by the command to fight, how can that be held possible? For, according to the law thus divinely enunciated, compulsion neutralises personal effort, destroys the grand object of religion, and cancels the merit and recompense resulting from free choice. And hence the divine law —LET THERE BE NO COMPULSION IN THE FAITH. But now, alas, for its reversal! The war-cry has drowned the word of peace. Compulsion supersedes the command against it, and the maxim, " I am not the Guardian over you," has vanished to the winds.

And here I may observe that, by introducing force and compulsion, Mohammed abrogated the first principle of conversion, namely, personal responsibility, with its spiritual recompense. How, then, can it be said that Mohammed "came as a Mercy to mankind," seeing that he hath deprived mankind, by the forcible imposition of Islam, of the grand virtue of personal effort and free choice, and the resulting recompense? In what way, my Friend, wilt thou escape from so manifest a contradiction, or reconcile two principles so diametrically opposed?

Now, I praise the Imâm for his desire to prove that none of the texts enjoining toleration have been cancelled. For he sees what every thinking man must see, namely, that it is impossible to abrogate them, since the prohibition against the use of force and against resort to compulsion, cannot be cancelled without destroying the chief purposes of religion and contravening the freedom of conscience, which is the gift of the Most High to mankind. Only, the Imâm fails to explain how abrogation is "far from being the case," or how virtual cancelment can be reconciled with the absence of the same. To do so is beyond the power of man.

VI. *If God had so pleased, they had not been Idolaters; and WE have not made thee to be Guardian over them, neither art thou their Keeper.*—SURA AL INÂM (vi.) v. 107.

Commentary on the latter clause—
When the Lord had made it clear that there was no other power but His own to put an end to unbelief, He completes the passage by showing to the Prophet what his duty was, namely, that He had not made him the Guardian of the people nor their Keeper in the way of interference. His simple duty was to deliver the divine commands and prohibitions in respect of doctrine and practice, explain the grounds of the message, and pronounce its sanctions. Those who accepted the same, the benefit was their own; and those who refused, the evil thereof rested on themselves.—*Râzi.*

And *Beidhawi*: We have not made thee a Watcher and Keeper over them that thou shouldest manage their affairs. Nor do thou upbraid those on whom they call besides the true God; that is, do not speak evil of the gods whom they worship.

Remarks.—This is now the sixth passage limiting the duty of Mohammed to that of a Messenger and Warner. Note, also, that it is to be the Prophet's answer to those who defied his mission; he is not to trouble them in any way, or interfere with the view of making them accept his faith; and that in three particulars—(1) by force of arms or other form of compulsion; (2) by withholding help or kindness from them; (3) by reviling them. The only remaining way was to warn them with kindness and benignity, whether they would hear or whether they would forbear.

VII. *If thy Lord had so willed, all upon the earth had believed, every one. Ah! wilt thou compel men to be believers, whereas no soul can believe but by the per-*

mission of God? And He will pour out His indignation on those that will not understand.—SURA YUNUS (x.) vv. 98, 99.

Commentary, by various authorities—

Had it been God's pleasure that force should have been used to lead men to the faith, He would have so decreed and legalised the same; but He hath not done so, because conversion which comes of compulsion is of no benefit to the convert. "Ah! wilt thou compel men to believe?" that is, thou hast no power to convert anyone. The effective power, and causative will, rest with the Almighty alone, for "no soul can believe without the permission of God." Saith the Cazee, Faith goeth not forth otherwise than by the knowledge of God and personal endeavour, or otherwise by the divine decree therefor.—*Rázi*.

Beidhawi: It is against the divine pleasure to use compulsion, which in itself cannot possibly attain the object. No one can believe but by the will of God; wherefore do not make the attempt, for that rests with God alone.

Remarks.—Doubtless the prohibition here made against the resort to force, like that in the first verse of this chapter, must have been due to Mohammed having either begun to use means of compulsion at the time, or having had it in his mind to do so when opportunity should offer. He is here reminded of the powerlessness of force to reach the goal of faith, which is the gift of God alone, and His prerogative. If compulsion be thus forbidden by God, whence came its introduction?

VIII. SAY, "*O men, the Truth hath now come unto you from your Lord! He, therefore, who is guided thereby is guided for* (*the benefit of*) *his own self; and he who goeth astray, for the same he goeth astray. And I am not the Master over you.*"—SURA YUNUS, Meccan, (x.) v. 106.

Commentary.—As if the Prophet were commanded to say, God hath perfected the divine law, and taken away every excuse and possible pretext. It is no business of mine to labour for your reward, or save you from your punishment, any more than I have done. Ibn Abbas says that the text is cancelled by the command to fight.—*Rázi.*

Remarks.—Observe two things. First, that the purpose of the Almighty in the mission of Mohammed was simply to reveal the divine law, so that he might place it before mankind; second, that no other commission was given him but to preach and warn. It follows that, when he proclaimed war and measures of violence, he was resorting to that which, being not the purpose of God in his mission, was wide of his duty. Now, seeing that his mission was so strictly confined within these limits, how could it have been lawful in him to smite and slay, to fight and raid and plunder, to take prisoners and make slaves? If such things were lawful, what are we to make of the command, "There shall be no force in religion"? What! art thou forcing men to believe? Compulsion, and yet no compulsion! By my life! one of the most extraordinary contradictions the world has ever heard; a conjunction of two principles absolutely irreconcilable. And how, O Ibn Abbas! is it admissible for thee to say that the text has been cancelled by the command to fight? Seest thou not that the prohibition of force is absolute; that to attempt forcible conversion is declared to be of no benefit, and contrary to the will of God? But, alas! this view of Ibn Abbas has become that of Moslems at large ever since the law of war appeared. How can they read the verses denouncing force, and yet give place in their heart to the command to fight? It is a mystery how the theologians of Islam can accept the eternal law of "no force in the faith," and at the same moment can see in the warlike passages both obligation and expediency. Holding thus both mandates to be from God, they are bewildered in a maze betwixt the one and the other, with no prospect of finding an escape.

IX. *They that have taken others besides Him as patrons, God observeth them; thou art not the Master over them.*—SURA SHÛRA, Meccan, (xlii.) v. 4.

    Commentary.—Those who worship, besides God, other gods, the Lord is Custodian over them and their affairs. Nothing escapeth Him. He it is that taketh account of them; there is none other but He alone. Thou, O Mohammed! hast no interest to meddle with their concerns, or compel them to enter the faith. Thou art but a Warner.—*Râzi.*

X. *It is God who hath made for you the things He hath created, conveniences of shade, and places of retreat in the mountains, and garments to defend you from the heat, and coats of mail as a defence in danger. Thus hath He fulfilled His favour towards you, that perchance ye may submit; but if they turn their backs, truly thy duty is but that alone of a plain Messenger. They recognise the favour of God, and then deny the same; and the most of them are Unbelievers.*—SURA AL NAKHL, Meccan, (lxviii.) vv. 78, 79.

    Commentary.—That is: If they turn back, O Mohammed! and, refusing thy call, prefer the pleasures of this present life, following their fathers in unbelief, they but incriminate their own

souls thereby. There is nothing further for thee to do but what thou art doing, namely, fully to deliver thy message.—*Râzi.*
Beidhawi to the same effect.

XI. *Whether we cause thee to see any part of that which WE have threatened them with, or cause thee first to die, verily, upon thee devolveth the message, and upon Us the reckoning.*—SURA AL RÁD, Medina, (xiii.) v. 40.

Commentary.—Whatever may happen in the future, thy duty is simply to deliver the command of the Lord, fulfilling thy trust and commission; with Us it rests to take account.

Remarks.—These three texts point to the same truth—(1) Whether the idolaters listened to the Book or went astray, Mohammed was not their keeper. It was no business of his to force them to the faith. (2) There was no keeper over them but God alone, in whose hands, not in the Prophet's, lay their destiny. (3) If the people rejected his summons, he had no further duty but to deliver the message. Strange that the learned doctors of Islam should have lost sight of the truth so explicitly set forth here, and have accepted in their stead the passages which they hold to have been revealed sanctioning war. If there be no keeper over the idolaters but God alone, how comest thou, O Mohammed, to assume that office over them; and, when forbidden to use force for their conversion, how camest thou to war against them, shed their blood, and carry off their wives and children captive? And, when commanded not to interfere with their affairs, but simply to deliver the message, whether they would hear or whether forbear, why didst thou not take thy stand within that limit, and leave them and their concerns to the Lord, with whom alone it rested? Or, as it is so plainly put in the third text, "With thee lies the message; with ME the reckoning."

XII. *And obey not the Unbelievers and the Hypocrites; and leave off harassing them. And put thy trust in God; for God is a sufficient protector.*—SURA AL AHZAB (xxxiii.) v. 45.

Commentary.—Obey not the Unbelievers; a reference to the Prophet's duty of warning and admonishing. And leave off annoying them; that is, leave it to God to punish them, either at your hands or by hell-fire.—*Râzi.*

Jelalein: "Leave off troubling them"; countenance not their infidelity and hypocrisy; but put thy trust in the Lord: He will suffice for thee.

Remarks.—It need not be wondered that Jelalein is here nearer the mark than Râzi, who is strangely at fault; for what intelligent reader would take the words "leave off harassing" the Unbelievers, to mean that the Unbelievers, instead of being left alone, might be punished at the hands of the Prophet and his followers? That is to say, prohibition to injure is, in Râzi's view, equal to an intimation of coming punishment at the hand of him who is prohibited from injuring them. In fact, Râzi would seem as if he saw no difference between such prohibition and the following command: "*They desire that ye should become disbelievers even as they are, and become like unto them. But take not from amongst them any friends, until they fly their country in the ways of God. But if they turn back, then seize them and slay them wheresoever ye find* them, and take not from amongst them any friend nor any helper"; [1] and this extraordinary meaning is got out of the text, "leave off harassing them"! He does not see that an agreement between these contradictory commands is about as great as an agreement between fire and water, between the forbidden and the lawful.

Again, observe how successive texts throw light on the apparent cause of their appearance. We have, first, "No compulsion in religion"; [2] then "Ah! wilt thou compel men to believe?" [3] And now, "Leave off harassing," which is a kind of compulsion. It would seem as if the Prophet had intended, or had even begun, to use such compulsory measures, when he was forbidden to use force. Then appeared the two verses repeating the prohibition; "Wilt thou compel?" and "Leave off harassing them,"—being a clear interdiction of what apparently had already been begun. Thus we see that prohibition follows prohibition, and injunction injunction, to the effect that Mohammed should not harass the idolaters or distress them with hostile acts, but confine himself to preaching and warning in a kindly way—بها في احسن. And here is ground for grave reflection.

XIII. *Do thou invite into the way of thy Lord by wisdom and mild exhortation, and dispute with them in the most gracious manner; for thy Lord well knoweth him that doth stray from His way, and He well knoweth them that are guided aright.*—SURA AL NAHL (xvi.) v. 123.

[1] Sura Al Nisa (iv.) v. 88. [2] P. 33. [3] P. 41.

Commentary.—The best and wisest around him are to be invited by wise and convincing evidence and discourse; the people at large by argument, reasonable, clear, and satisfying; while even the contentious are to be reasoned with in the most excellent and perfect way. "The Lord knoweth those that are guided aright"; that is, busy thyself in summoning people to the Lord in these three ways, for the result, *i.e.* in men choosing the right, appertaineth not unto thee.—*Râzi.*

And *Jelalein*: Call men, O Mohammed, unto the way of the Lord by wisdom, that is, by the Coran, and kindly discourse, and friendly words; and dispute in the way that is most attractive, that is, by the Word of God and by argument; "for the Lord knoweth him that shall go astray," and will recompense the same.

Remarks.—This text explains the office of the Prophet. He was to summon those around him to the faith, by proofs and evidence, in a mild and friendly way; and within these limits to restrain his action. Would that Mohammed had held by the procedure thus enjoined, and taken his stand on the boundary here laid down; and not, following in the footsteps of his enemies (as Kab ibn Ashraf, Abu Afak, Sofian ibn Khalid, Abu Rafi, etc.), overstepped that limit into the domain of war and treachery; a line of action unworthy of any brave man, how much more of one that professed to be a prophet sent to teach and guide mankind!

XIV. *WE have revealed it (the Coran) with the truth, and with the truth it hath descended; and WE have not sent thee otherwise than as a bearer of good tidings and a Warner.*—SURA ISRAEL (xvii.) v. 104.

Commentary.—The preceding passage speaks of the Coran as a miracle and the evidence thereof. Then it is related how the Unbelievers, not accepting it as such, demanded other kind of miracles; to which God replied that there was not any need for such, and established it by many reasons. One is, that Moses showed nine miracles, and that when the people nevertheless contended with him, God destroyed them. And so it was here. If Mohammed were to show his people such miracles as they demanded, and they denied them, they would have become liable to the same doom of extermination; but that, again, would not have been permissible, seeing that God foreknew that amongst them were such as should thereafter believe; and that even of those who might not, there would still arise a believing progeny. The passage then returns to the glorification of the Coran, and its perfection as having been "sent down with the truth"; that is, its grand purpose hath been to establish the truth and righteousness.

The text proceeds to say that Mohammed was not sent but as a Messenger of good and a Warner, thus :—These ignorant people who demand miracles and refuse thy religion, these are not in any wise responsible for their infidelity; for WE have not sent thee otherwise than as a bringer of good tidings to the obedient, and as a Warner to them that are rebellious. If they accept the faith, it is for their own benefit; if they refuse, their infidelity is no business of thine.—*Râzi.*

Remarks.—The questions whether the Coran is a miracle, and why miracles are withheld, lest the rejecters should be destroyed, have been disposed of in the first chapter. And so I would only ask my gentle reader's attention to the words "*not otherwise*" in the text. "WE have not sent thee otherwise than as a preacher and a warner." This is the answer which the prophet gives as coming from heaven to those who demanded miracles like those of Moses and Jesus. Mohammed, the verse says, was not sent to perform miracles; his office embraced two things only, namely, to bring good tidings and to warn; "not otherwise"; a distinct limit not to be overpassed. And I ask any intelligent person whether the Prophet was not directly prohibited in this and other similar passages from overstepping the clear boundary here marked out for him, and irrevocably fixed by the words "not otherwise"?

Now, how was it possible for men to recognise in Mohammed the simple preacher and warner, when they saw him soon after become the fierce warrior and imperious autocrat, summoning those around him at the point of the sword to accept his religion, or "pay tribute with the hand, and be in subjection"? Where is the connection between two such opposing commands,—said to emanate both from the same Almighty hand,—one absolutely limiting the Prophet's duty to preaching and warning, the other launching him forth at the head of armies to force the acceptance of Islam? Can any intelligent Moslem, free to think and judge for himself, read the one set of positive and peremptory limitations, and then without being utterly embarrassed and confounded, contemplate his Prophet as a man of war and conquest, havoc, spoil, and rapine? No, by my life, No!

XV. *Verily, WE have revealed unto thee the Book with truth; he that is guided thereby, it is for his own soul; and he that erreth, he erreth for the same; and thou art not over them a Master.* — SURA ZAMR, Meccan, (xxxix.) v. 41.

Commentary.—Mohammed being distressed at the persistence of his people in unbelief, is told by the Almighty that the perfect and glorious Book had been sent down a blessing and guide unto mankind, itself the Truth and a miracle proving its own divine origin; that whether men followed its guidance or went astray, it was their own matter; he was not guardian over them. "Thou art not set to drive them to the faith in the way of force and violence;

its acceptance or rejection is their own affair,"—all which was meant to console the Prophet in his distress at their persistence in unbelief.—*Râzi.*

Remarks.—The last six verses, taken from five different Suras, are all to the same effect, that Mohammed was forbidden to use compulsion or constraint towards Unbelievers. He was not their master to impose his own will and commands upon them; force, moreover, we are told, destroys the virtue of conversion. God was the Master; it rested with Him to guide, and with Him to take account. Man was free to accept the faith or to refuse. Mohammed was not "over them a Master." Such is the strenuously reiterated sense of the texts and of the commentaries thereon.

The conclusions from the passages quoted in this chapter may be thus summed up—(1) the unlawfulness of compulsion in religion; (2) or of interfering with those who refused the call of Mohammed; (3) the impropriety of even withholding alms from such; and (4) the Prophet's work was to preach and warn, and that alone. Now consider, when Mohammed was not only forbidden to use coercion towards his opponents, but commanded to show them kindness,—even to the extent of not withholding alms, lest the refusal might be held an inducement to conversion, and lest such action should detract from the merit of voluntary conversion;—after all these plain and stringent inhibitions, was any possible plea left for the passages which enjoin fighting and resort to force? Never! How shall there be no constraint in the faith, and yet constraint; compulsion neutralising virtue, and the virtue yet remain; Mohammed sent without these things, yet sent with them? By my life! could any contradictions transcend these? They are absolutely irreconcilable.

How is it conceivable to attribute inconsistency such as this to the Most High; that He should say, " I have sent My servant to such a work," and, again, " I have sent him for a work directly opposed thereto";—forbidden His servant as wrong a certain line of action, and then commanded him to do what He had just forbidden; prohibited the use of force and compulsion towards the unbelievers and the hypocrites, and then appointed His servants to fight against such, even to the death? Impossible! God forbid that we should speak thus of the Most High and Holy One!

REVIEW

The mild and tolerant precepts reviewed in this chapter were acted on by Mohammed, so long as he lived at Mecca, in a kindly, gentle, and forbearing spirit; and so, likewise, for a time after his flight to Yathreb. But so soon as he had gained power there, and found himself supported by a host of warriors ready at his call, he saw it expedient to turn aside from the paths of peace and moderation into those of war, maraud, and plunder. From the messenger of good tidings and simple warner, he changed into the champion and the autocrat; from the man of peace, into the man of war and rapine. Once begun, forays, raids, battles, and campaigns followed fast on one another; and we might even have doubted that words of peace had ever proceeded from his lips, if we had not found them still there in the Coran.

The question of cancelment, that is, of opposing verses, abrogating one the other, is reserved for a separate chapter. I would here only ask the thoughtful and unprejudiced Moslem, whether he does not see that the doctrine laid down in these verses, forbidding force and constraint in religion, is an obligation for all time,—one of those moral principles which cannot be abrogated, but must last as long as the world itself. Such being the case, running counter to it by action directly its opposite, is running counter to what is eternally right. Can that be? And if not, who will help us out of the labyrinth? True, some Commentators, as we have seen, avoid the difficulty by holding that the tolerant commands of the Coran were intended by their Divine Author to be of only temporary duration. But this, as every impartial thinker must see, is an utterly untenable assumption. If any Believer, out of desire to preserve the harmony of his Scripture, should hold this view, one can only say that he does violence to his sense of right and wrong; for the very passages which enjoin toleration are amongst the most weighty and dominant in the Coran, and the principle they over and over inculcate beyond the possibility of recall,—a perpetual rule of human obligation.

How can the enlightened and impartial Moslem believe that these commands were sent down to be observed by the Prophet only so long as he was in a weak and helpless condition, and to be cast aside the moment he became great amongst men, possessed of resources, and surrounded by followers, while all the time there was before his eyes, as in great letters of gold—

LET THERE BE NO COMPULSION IN THE FAITH.

WE have not sent thee but as a Messenger of good tidings and a Warner.

To thee belongeth the message; to Us the account.

How is the intelligent Believer to find his way here? If such commands be held, as they must needs be held, binding and obligatory, where is the room for the passages commanding war against the Unbelievers, compulsion to join the faith, and vengeance against those who refuse? Can we reconcile the two sets of passages, the tolerant and the hostile? And if not, how can both have proceeded from the Almighty? You endeavour to cut the Gordian knot by saying, "Praise be to the Lord, the Glorious and All-wise; He knoweth that which we know not." Yes; praise be to the Lord, now and evermore!—only, to praise God, and exalt His holy name, is one thing, and to understand aright these verses, their bearing, and the bringing them into practice, is quite a different thing. The Lord guide His servants by His grace and mercy into that which is right and in accordance with His glory! He is over all things supreme, and He is worthy to be praised.

CHAPTER III

PASSAGES IN THE CORAN THAT CANCEL, AND PASSAGES THAT ARE CANCELLED

1. *Whatever verse WE cancel, or cause thee to forget, WE will give a better than it, or one like thereunto. What! dost thou not know that God is over all things powerful?*—SURA BACR (ii.) v. 102.

Commentary.—It was one of the taunts of the Jews, "See ye not that Mohammed gives a command to his Companions, and then withdrawing it, gives a directly opposite one? He says one thing to-day, and next day revokes it." Whereupon this was revealed.

That some passages are cancelled by others, admits of several proofs. *First*, There is the present verse. *Second*, The period before which a widow can marry again was changed from a year to four months and ten days. *Third*, The verse, that "twenty of you if steadfast shall beat two hundred," that is to say, in the proportion of one to ten, was cancelled by another verse which, recognising that some were weak, lightened the burden thus: "If there be one hundred steadfast amongst you, they shall beat two hundred," or in the proportion of one to two. *Fourth*, The Haram of Mekka cancelled the former Kibla of Jerusalem. And so that passage, "When WE change one verse for another, they say, Verily thou art a forger." The cancelled passage may be either taken away or it may be left in its place. It may also have been caused to be forgotten before being recorded (as we are told of a Sura which, recited overnight, had passed altogether from the memory by next morning), so that the whole passage disappeared from the Coran, and thus also from being used in recitation or at prayer. It may also be that a command has been cancelled, while the passage containing it remains in the Book, and continues to be read.—*Râzi*.

So also *Beidhawi*: The Jews and Idolaters said, "Look at Mohammed; he gives an order to his followers, and then tells them exactly the opposite"; on which this verse was revealed. Cancelment consists either in removing the verse itself or abrogating what it commands, or both together. "WE cancel," that is, WE command thee, or Gabriel, in respect of its abrogation, and thou shalt find it cancelled.

Abdullah has this various reading: "Whatever WE cause thee to forget, or cancel it, WE bring thee a better than it"; that is, one which brings greater benefit and reward, or the like thereof. "Knowest thou not that God is powerful over all things?"; that is, hath the power to cancel, and to give the like of what is cancelled, or better? This verse proves that cancelment is to be held as existing in the Coran.

And *Jelalein*: "Cancel"; that is, cancel it in the heavenly Table. "Cause thee to forget"; that is, wipe it out of thy heart. "A better"; that is, a simpler and easier verse, or one bringing greater reward. "Or like it"; that is, in what it imposes, or the reward it brings. "Over all things powerful"; that is, as in other things, so also here, able to cancel and change, or to alter the sense.

For the rest, as above.

Remarks.—I. Observe, first, the complaints of the Idolaters and Jews; what impartial person will not recognise the reasonableness of their objection? For, as regard the Arabs, they are as famous for standing by their word as for their generosity; they would die rather than change. So when they saw Mohammed going back from what he had once said, authorising to-day what he had prohibited the day before, they took amiss a practice so foreign to Arabian wont, and refused to accept the faith of Islam, which they held responsible for it.

So also as regards the Jews scandalised at change or cancelment; they had never heard anything of the kind either in their Law or Prophets. For no command or prohibition in the Law as given by Moses was ever cancelled either by Moses himself, or by Joshua his successor. And all the prophets that followed, even to the days of Jesus, observed the Law as it was revealed to Moses without change or variation. So when the Jews saw Mohammed, who laid claim to the gift of prophecy, cancelling not merely the commands of the Tourât, but many of the commands which he professed himself to have received from God, and that in order to suit the exigencies of day and place, they denied his pretensions, looking upon them as the mere expedients of a secular government.

II. Again, resort to change and cancelment is a mark of defective power; and far be it from the Almighty that there should be sign of weakness in His dealings, for a work showing weakness can be none of His. In one example given us, the interval before which a widow could not remarry was shortened, as if the reason for so shortening it was not known before. In the next, the change is in the number required to rout the enemy,—the proportion being increased fivefold in view of God's knowledge as to weakness amongst them, as if that had not been known to the Almighty before!

III. As to the forgotten passages, some hold that they were altogether obliterated; others, that their purport was cancelled, but not their recitation; others, again, hold to both kinds of abrogation under the repeated "or" in the text;—"Or, We cause thee (Mohammed or Gabriel) to forget." Of the various modes of obliteration from the memory or from the Coran, of the text itself or of its purport, or of both, I would ask my reader which he adopts; and where the cancelled verses remain in the Coran, how is it that they continue to be recited while their force and purport no longer hold good?

Again, "We shall make it forgotten" would signify the obliviousness of the hearer or reader,—in fact, that he became as if he had never heard it,—which hardly accords with the tradition that the people read a Sura to-day, and by the morning had forgotten all about it. And if the cancelled verses continued in the Coran, and so were read heard and understood, what does the "cause it to be forgotten" mean, when it was not forgotten? Supposing now that this passage was intended (as we are told) to silence the Jews and to satisfy the Companions, the matter becomes stranger still, for what is there in it at all likely to have such an effect? And now consider, in thus removing parts of the law and supplying their place by others, "the like thereof or better," what evidence is there of the miraculous? "True," you reply, "but knowest thou not that God is over all things powerful?" Rather, is not all this a sign of the weakness of the creature, who seeks to improve his work by revising it throughout by changes and alterations; and that just as is the wont of authors from amongst mankind?

II. *And when WE substitute one verse in place of another verse (and God best knoweth that which He revealeth) they say, "Thou art nothing but a forger." Nay, but the most of them know not. SAY, "The Holy*

Spirit hath revealed it from thy Lord with truth, to stablish them that do believe, and as a guide and good tidings unto the Moslems." — SURA AL NAHL (xvi.) vv. 99, 100.

Commentary.—Ibn Abbas tells us that when a severe revelation came from heaven, and shortly after a more lenient one, the unbelieving Coreish would say, "Truly, Mohammed maketh sport of his followers; to-day he giveth an order and the next day forbiddeth it; he saith these things simply out of his own head"; whereupon this passage was revealed.

"Changing one verse for another" means taking away something and putting something else in its place, or cancelling one verse by another. "God best knoweth,"—He is acquainted with what presses heavily, and what lightly, upon His servants, and with their wants, modifying the revelation accordingly,—which is an answer to the taunt of the Unbelievers, that the Prophet was "a forger." "But most of them know not"; that is, are ignorant of the real nature of the Coran, and the advantage of changes and cancelment for the benefit of His servants.

"The Holy Spirit," that is, Gabriel, brought down the Coran from thy Lord, to stablish the Believers, and satisfy them in this matter of cancelment. Abu Muslim (Ispahany school) alone holds that there is no such thing as cancelment in the Moslem law, the reference here being to the abrogation of something in the text of the former Scriptures,—as the change of the Kibla from Jerusalem to the Kaaba,—for which change the Unbelievers called the Prophet "a forger." But the Commentators, without exception, hold that cancelment has its place in the present law. Shafei, again, says that no text in the Coran can be cancelled by the Sunnat, basing this view on the text, "When WE change one verse *by another verse.*" But this argument cannot be based upon the text; and besides, Gabriel revealed the Sunnat as well as the Coran.—*Kázi.*

Beidhawi: The cancelling verse takes the place of the cancelled both in word and authority. "The Lord best knoweth what is revealed"—that is, of its expediency; what might be expedient at one time might be hurtful afterwards, and then it would be cancelled; so also, what might not be expedient now might become so thereafter, and take its place. "They say thou art a forger," palming off things of thine own on God; now issuing an order, and then, having changed thy mind, countermanding it, the answer being, "The Lord best knoweth, but most of them know not"; they know not the reason of such commands, nor can distinguish the wrong from the right.

Jelalein: "When WE change one verse for another," that is, cancel it, and reveal a different one for the benefit of Thy servants, they say to the Prophet, "Thou art a forger"—a liar; that is, thou sayest just what is thine own. "But most of them understand not"; that is, the true sense of the Coran and advantage of the cancelment.

Remarks.—The text contains no satisfactory answer to the objections of the unbelieving Coreish. They said that Mohammed trifled with his followers, giving out as revelations from God things that came out of his own head—"forgeries," as, in fact, they called them; and this both because of frequent abrogation and change, and his failing to give any proof of the Coran, and of the cancelled passages, being a divine communication. The text simply denies the charge, and asserts that the Coran is brought down from heaven by Gabriel; but as his opponents said that the Coran was Mohammed's own composition, this simple assertion, also from himself, left the accusation just where it was.

The Commentators justify cancelment because "of the advantage of the change so made for the benefit of His servants."[1] True, both sides saw that the changes were made for some object. The Arabs did not deny that there was advantage to Mohammed in the war, rapine, and victories sanctioned by such change; what they did complain of was that the new commands were diametrically opposed to the far more

[1] Râzi, p. 59.

numerous passages in which the Almighty was represented as absolutely prohibiting resort to force, as shown in the second chapter. Their objection, in short, was that they saw the Prophet changing the Coran so as to suit the expediency and exigencies of the moment, and concluded that it was therefore the creation of his own mind; for, had it come from the Almighty, it would not have been cancelled and altered simply to meet the varying motions of the human heart. And so it might be said that the Coran followed the Moslems, not the Moslems the Coran. As if the great God, dependent on the will of His servants, withdrew to-day from the command of yesterday, and changed His word at the will, desires, and inclinations of the creature. Far exalted is the Lord Almighty above such a thought! As for man, the creature of change and circumstance, weak and sinful, to suppose that the Almighty cancels and alters His word, making that lawful now which He had before declared unlawful, to suit the inclination of the creature and the expediency of the day, is nothing but to forge a lie against Him. How could it be otherwise? He is the All-wise, unchangeable in word, steadfast in design. He unfoldeth to the creature His will, and revealeth unto mankind His commands,—all in accord with the infinite perfections and unapproachable greatness of His divine nature. He is not a man that He should lie, or the son of man that He should repent. Shall He say, and not bring it to pass? Glory be to Him, with whom there is neither change nor the shadow of turning!

III. *Those of your women who commit immorality, let four of you be brought to witness against them; and if they bear witness, then shut them up in apartments until death release them, or God make a way for them.*—SURA AL NISA, Medina, (iv.) v. 14.

Commentary.—It is thought that this text was cancelled by a verbal command (Hadith) to the following effect: The Prophet cried aloud,—" Come, listen to me; listen to me! God hath 'made a way' both for the maiden and the married woman. The maiden shall be scourged and sent away; the married woman, scourged and stoned to death." Afterwards the Hadith also was cancelled by the word of God (in the Coran),—" The adulteress and the adulterer, let both be scourged with an hundred stripes." According to this view, the text in the Coran was cancelled by the Sunnat (Hadith); and again the Sunnat cancelled by a second text. Others hold that the text was cancelled by the verse commanding stripes instead. Such is the view of one set of Commentators.

Abu Bekr Al Râzi, from his intense opposition to Al Shafei, says: The first interpretation is the right one; for if the verse enjoining stripes had preceded the Prophet's call, " Come, listen to me," that call could have had no meaning. We must therefore hold that the Prophet's call preceded the verse commanding stripes. And for the same reason, the verse enjoining imprisonment was cancelled by the Hadith; and likewise the Hadith was cancelled by the verse enjoining stripes. Hence it follows that the Coran and the Sunnat may both be cancelled, the one by the other.

Other Commentators again, differing from Abu Bekr Al Râzi, hold that the meaning of the first verse is, that sinning women must be "shut up in apartments until the Lord should make a way of escape"; "the way" being thus left to be determined in the future. Then followed the Prophet's command, that the married woman was to be stoned, etc.; which was, in fact, "the way" promised in the text, not the cancelling of it. It might even be held that this Hadith refers to both, being an explanation specially of the one verse, and generally of the other, thus avoiding the necessity of repeated cancelment.

The school of Abu Hanifa hold that the text commanding imprisonment was cancelled by that commanding stripes.—*Râzi.*

Remarks.—This verse, with its commentary, is incredibly strange; the Coran cancelled by the Sunnat, and the Sunnat by the Coran: a chase, as it were, between the two. It is held that the text was cancelled by the Sunnat (Hadith), "Come, listen to me," etc., as we have seen; and, again, that the Coran asserted its authority, cancelling the Sunnat by the verse ordering stripes instead.[1]

It is as if the Coran and Hadith were, in respect of this question, at variance, desiring each to discredit the other. Some seek to escape from the dilemma by making the oral command in the Hadith to be, in fact, "the way" promised in the text,—that is, appointing stripes for the maiden, and stoning for the married woman. Will this satisfy the sincere and thoughtful Moslem? He will not fail to note that the text, which lays down imprisonment as the punishment for immoral women, is abrogated by the later text, which substitutes stripes. Now, if "the way" promised in the former text be (according to the Hadith) stoning, then the subsequent verse substituting stripes must be held again to cancel the Hadith; so that the Hadith, which prescribes stoning, cannot be "the way" promised in the text. Now consider (and the Lord guide thee aright!) what all this implies. Does action of the kind here described become the great and all-wise Creator? Is it not derogatory to His perfections that He should say one thing and then cancel it by a different order,

---

[1] *Sunnat* is the law derived from the practice or sayings of the Prophet. *Hadith* is the tradition embodying the same.

and again cancel the repealing order by a third? Would this become any of the great men of the earth? Never! Hast thou ever heard of behaviour like this in the Princes of this world? And if it would not be becoming in the creature, how much more incompatible with the Lord of heaven and earth! Far exalted is He above such infirmity. High and mighty beyond such imputation!

REVIEW

There is nothing that more perplexes the thoughtful Believer of the day than this question of parts of the divine revelation cancelling other parts; and the uneasiness is all the greater when he sees the purpose for which the changes were made. Can such a one shut his eyes to the fact that the passages cancelled contain instructions highly expedient for the interests of the day, the Moslems being at the moment in a weak and dependent state; and that what is substituted in their stead, of war and force, was equally expedient for Islam and the government of Mohammed when he became strong and powerful? Is it possible to see any way out of the difficulty when one has ever before his eyes the absolute command revealed over and again at Mecca, while Islam was yet depressed;—" We have not sent thee otherwise than as a Messenger and a Warner"?[1] No, by my life! And again, what is equally perplexing, namely, the inability to determine which is the command that

[1] Sura Israel (Mecca), v. 104.

cancels and which the one cancelled; possibly that which cancels might, for all that is in the Coran, be held by me to be the one cancelled or the reverse. For example, how can I tell whether the command, "Let there be no compulsion in the Faith,"[1] does not cancel the passages authorising compulsion? and, indeed, some of the Commentators, as we have seen, do construe the passage as a continuing prohibition having a perpetual force in matters of religion.[2] But if not, I would ask what was the occasion for the repeated prohibition of force, seeing that Mohammed was preceded by Jesus, son of Mary, who, as all men know, was himself gentle and gracious to all around, preached love and benevolence to the multitudes who followed him, and left this command to his apostles and people, "Love your enemies: do good to them that hate you; and treat them that despitefully use you with pity and forbearance." Now, if, on the contrary, Jesus had come forcing men unto the faith, and Mohammed appeared a mercy to mankind, there might have been reason for the revelation, "Let there be no force in religion," as a warning to avoid the ways of his predecessor, and confine himself to the simple duty of a Messenger and Warner. But as Jesus never taught the use of force, the reiterated command could have had no reference to the past dispensation, and must therefore be regarded as an embargo addressed to Mohammed, forbidding him to do something which he was in danger of doing. And what throws a suggestive

[1] Sura Al Bakr, v. 252. [2] See above, Chap. II. p. 33.

light on the occasion is that other passage: "Ah! wilt thou compel (or art thou compelling[1]) men to believe, while it appertaineth to no one to believe but by permission of God alone?" Now what reason can be assigned for this, but that the Prophet had already begun to use force, or desired to do so? and thus it became necessary to forbid him, which was done by the numerous passages enjoining toleration quoted in the foregoing chapter. It follows that the cancelment of this prohibition by the subsequent command legalising force (nothing in the way of compulsion having as yet taken place), shows that the foregoing passages were really a prohibition of what Mohammed desired, or possibly was already beginning to do. And so when the prohibition was cancelled, the above text remained as it were standing between the two sets of contradictory commands. The course may thus be conceived: when the desire to use force and impose tribute began to stir in the Prophet's breast, or to be tried in practice, then came the texts prohibiting such compulsion; and so, for a time, it was given up, and resort had only to "preaching and warning," until the desire returned overpoweringly upon him; and then no longer able to forbear, he cancelled the prohibition of force, and legalised, by the new law, resort to war. Thenceforward the course before prohibited became the course he was commanded to pursue: that which had been declared contrary to right principles and spiritual

---

[1] Sura Yunas (x.) vv. 97, 98 افانت تكره الناس حتى يومنون.

benefit, declared to be directly in accord with both.

In illustration, will the reader consider what principles could be more irreconcilable than these, "Let there be no compulsion in the Faith," compared with "Fight against them till opposition cease, and the Faith be the Lord's alone";[1] "Fight in the way of God against them that fight against you, and transgress not; for God loveth not the transgressors";[2] "When the sacred months shall have passed, then slay the heathen wheresoever ye find them";[3] and "When ye meet the Unbelievers, strike off their heads until ye have made great slaughter amongst them, and bind them in bonds," and so on.[4]

Also these texts: "Say unto those who have received the Scriptures, and to the heathen, *Will ye believe?* Now, if they believe (*i.e.* accept Islam), they are guided aright; but if they turn their backs, thou hast but to deliver thy message, for God watcheth over His servants";[5] contrasted with,— "Fight against those who believe not in God and in the Last day, who forbid not that which God and His Prophet have forbidden, and who follow not the true religion, from amongst the people of the Book, until they pay tribute with their hand, and are abased."[6]

Also this: "Obey not the Unbelievers and the Hypocrites, and leave off troubling them; and place

---

[1] Sura Baer (ii.) 188.
[2] *Ibid.* 185.
[3] Sura Al Tauba (ix.) 5.
[4] Sura Mohammed (xlvii.) 4.
[5] Sura Al Imran (iii.) 18.
[6] Sura Al Tauba (ix.) 28.

thy trust in God, for He is a sufficient guardian";[1] with—"They would that ye should disbelieve, even as they disbelieve, and that ye should become like unto them; wherefore, take no friend from amongst them until they fly their country in the way of God; but if they turn their back, lay hold of them and slay them wheresoever ye find them, and take not from amongst them any friend nor any helper";[2] and "O Prophet! wage war against the infidels and the hypocrites, and lay thy hand heavy upon them: their home shall be hell, a miserable end."[3]

Compare again these: "We have not sent thee otherwise than as a preacher of good tidings and a warner";[4] "Thy duty is to bear the message, Ours to take the account,"[5] and "Thou art not their master";[6] with the following, " Fight in the way of the Lord; cumber none other than thine own self, and stir up the Believers (to battle)";[7] and "O Prophet! stir up the Faithful to fight; if there be twenty steadfast men among you, they shall conquer two hundred," and so on.[8] Such passages abound, and one need quote no more.

To maintain the harmony of the Coran against the imputation of contradiction or discrepancy, it is held (as we have seen) that one set of these passages is abrogated by the other, namely, that the former were meant to be effective but for a limited term, and that

---

[1] Sura Al Ahzab (xxxiii.) 45.   [2] Sura Al Nisa (iv.) 88.
[3] Sura Al Tauba (ix.) 71, and Sura Tahrim (lxvi.) 11.
[4] Sura Israil (xvii.) 104.   [5] Sura Al Rád (xiii.) 40.
[6] Sura Shora (xlii.) 4.   [7] Sura Al Nisa (iv.) 83.
[8] Sura Al Anfal (viii.) 65.

this term was closed by the new revelation which cancelled it, and brought in a new order of things. When one asks for proof, we are referred to the cancelling text as divine authority for the change. But where is the proof of the cancelling text being divine? Is it in accordance with reason to suppose that a course of action should be prohibited which before was enjoined, and a new course commanded which before was interdicted, and both by the same divine authority? Can it be conceived that the entire Coran, composed of such discordant materials, should be from God? And if one inquires, Which is the cancelled command and which the text that, cancelling it, brings it to its appointed end?—there is no authoritative reply, when it is seen that, in the verse said to be cancelled, there exists precisely the same power of annulment as in the verse which is said to cancel. How, then, is the simple reader of the Coran to know whether the text, "There shall be no compulsion in the faith," and its fellows, do not in reality cancel the verses directing compulsion, rather than that they are cancelled by them? I cannot conceive how any intelligent Believer is able to reconcile his mind to accept the abrogation of such distinct and absolute prohibition of constraint, and of all approach to coercion and intolerance. How much more, then, with others than Moslems, who see at once that the transformation is in the Person, not in the Word; that the wish to change the method changed the command; that the longing after war and its spoils led to the supersession of the texts of peace and toleration by those enjoining the use of arms; that thus the preacher and man of peace became the warrior and the man of violence; the Bearer of good tidings, the intolerant Dictator.

And what makes this all the more remarkable is, that the act sometimes preceded the repealing text which sanctioned it, not the text the act; that is to say, the command was transgressed prior to its being cancelled; the transgression itself being, in fact, the occasion of the repeal of the command transgressed. The expedition of Abdallah ibn Jahsh to Nakhla affords an apt illustration.[1] The text which cancels the prohibition of war in the Sacred month is as follows: "They will ask thee concerning the Sacred month, whether they may war therein. SAY, Warring therein is grievous; but to obstruct the way of God, that is more grievous with God," etc.[2] Observe that this sanction was revealed *after* Abdallah had made his murderous raid on the Coreishite travellers who were halting, secure in the sacredness of the season; *after* the fifth of the booty had reached Medina; and *after* the complaint of the Coreish, and the disquiet of the Companions at the breach of the inviolate month. The cancelling order followed the act which it legalised, did not precede it,—a fact to be noted. There are many other instances of the change following the occasion, or the wish for it. Take that of the transfer of the Kibla from Jerusalem to the Kaaba.[3] We are told that Mohammed greatly

---

[1] *Life of Mahomet*, p. 201.   [2] Sura Baer (ii.) v. 217, and Râzi.
[3] *Life of Mahomet*, p. 183.

longed for this change, and then came this revelation, "Verily WE have observed thee turning about toward the heavens; wherefore WE shall cause thee to turn thyself toward a Kibla that shall please thee. Turn thy face, therefore, towards the Masjid al Harâm; wheresoever ye be turn your faces towards it."[1] Thus we see that when Mohammed was not pleased with the *Beit ul Makdas* of the Jews as the Kibla of his Arab followers, but, for objects of State desired to substitute the Haram of Mecca as the spot to which they should turn in prayer, the change was made in accordance with his wish.

Another similar instance of a revelation following the desire for it, is that of the Prophet's marriage with Zeinab, wife of Zeid, his adopted son.[2] Having accidentally seen this lady in scanty attire, Mohammed was smitten by her beauty. "Good Lord!" he exclaimed, "that turneth the hearts of men"; and he desired to marry her if he could find a way to avoid the scandal. Thereupon the following verse sanctioning the marriage appeared: "And when thou saidst to him on whom God had bestowed favour, and on whom thou too hadst bestowed favours, *Keep thy wife to thyself, and fear God*; and didst conceal in thy heart that which God was minded to make known; and thou fearedst man, whereas God is more worthy to be feared; and when Zeid had fulfilled her divorce, WE joined thee with her in marriage," so on to the end of the verse.[3]

[1] Sura Baer (ii.) v. 146, and Râzi. [2] *Life of Mahomet*, p. 281.
[3] Sura Ahzab (xxxiii.) 236, and Râzi.

A dispensation was granted from Heaven to the followers of the Prophet, who were allowed to consort with their wives during the fast, thus: "It is lawful on the nights of the fast to go in unto your wives. They are a garment unto you, and you are a garment unto them. God knoweth that ye are defrauding yourselves, wherefore He hath turned unto you and forgiven you. Now, therefore, consort with them";—and so on to the end of the verse.[1] We are told that at first such an indulgence was not lawful to the Moslems, according to the Jewish institution, on the fast being thus prescribed:—"A fast is appointed, as it was to those before you";[2] and that the restraint was removed by the above verse. There are other traditions about this matter, but they are hardly fit to be mentioned here.

Another not very attractive passage is that which relates to an oath which Mohammed had imposed on himself, and is as follows: "O Prophet, why dost thou forbid thyself that which God hath made lawful unto thee, seeking to please thy wives? and God is forgiving and merciful. Verily, God hath made lawful unto you the unloosing of your oaths; and God is your Master. He is the Knowing and the Wise."[3] The occasion was in this wise. Haphsa, daughter of Omar, being absent from her house, the Prophet took advantage of the occasion to company with Mary, his Coptic slave-girl, in Haphsa's chamber; when she, returning unexpectedly, surprised them thus together; and the affront was very grievous to her. On this

---

[1] Sura Bacr (ii.) v. 188, and Râzi.   [2] *Ibid.* v. 184.
[3] Sura Tahrim (lxvi.) vv. 1, 2.

the Prophet pacified her, and begged her to hide the matter. He also engaged to forego entirely the company of Mary, and gave her other promises regarding the advancement of her father. But Haphsa went and told Ayesha; and so, when the scandal got abroad, the Prophet separated from her, and retired also from the society of his other wives for nine and twenty days, until (as they say) Gabriel descended and bade him recall Haphsa, as she was a good woman, fasting and upright. According to Masruc, the passage making lawful the breaking of oaths had reference to the Prophet's promise to Haphsa, when he forbade himself the society of his Omm Walad (Mary the Coptic maid), and swore that he would not again approach her; from which oath he was thus set free. The reader will observe that Mohammed, having renounced further intercourse with Mary, confirmed it by an oath; and that he subsequently separated from Haphsa. But he could not bear the separation long, and, moreover, regretted having divorced the daughter of his friend Omar. Still, for a prophet to do that which would have been unlawful in others lay heavy on his mind, until this verse was revealed sanctioning his return to Mary, the oath notwithstanding; and then the message conveyed by Gabriel restored Haphsa to her position as his wife. Comment on all this is hardly needed.

The following narrative is also in point. At the siege of the Beni Nadhir (a Jewish tribe close to Yathreb), Mohammed caused the date trees round their village to be destroyed,—a practice repugnant to the Jewish law.¹ On this the Jews cried aloud from their battlements: "O Mohammed, thou wert wont to forbid injustice and rebuke the perpetrator thereof; wherefore then hast thou cut down our date trees, and burned them with fire? Dost thou call that the wrong or the right?" The thing also displeased the Companions, who were touched by the appeal of the besieged. Thereupon the following justification appeared: "That which thou didst cut down of the date trees,² or left standing upon their roots, it was by the command of God, that He might abase the evil-doers."³

We may here notice a passage of another nature, said to have declared an act of the Prophet's to have been unlawful, namely, his having prayed over the grave of the hypocrite⁴ Abdallah ibn Abi Salul, and forbidding him to do anything of the kind for the future. The text is, "And do not thou ever pray over any of them that may die, nor stand over his grave; for they have denied God and His Prophet, and die in their wickedness."⁵ The text, we are told, was revealed just at the moment when Mohammed had finished the prayer over Abdallah's body, and was standing by his grave to see it filled up. Others say that Omar having counselled the Prophet not to pray over the body of Abdallah on account of his hypocrisy, and he not consenting thereto, this passage

---

¹ Râzi; see also *Life of Mahomet*, p. 273.
² لينة the fine date of Medina having no stone.
³ Sura Al Hashar (lix.) v. 5.
⁴ Hypocrite, *i.e.* outwardly a Believer, but at heart an infidel.
⁵ Sura Al Tauba (ix.) v. 86.

was revealed confirming the view of Omar; as was also the case in passages supporting Omar's advice in respect of the Kibla, the curtaining of women, and the prohibition of wine.[1]

And now reflect (and may the Lord guide thee!) on the kind of wants and attractions, desires and actions, which led to revelations such as these. By my life! hast thou ever met with the like thereof in the Tourât; that the Lord should cancel any one of His commandments, or make that lawful which He had forbidden, in order to sanction transgression of law or breach of faith, or hath promulgated laws to meet man's desires, or to satisfy his inclinations or passion, be it for an individual or a people, for a prophet or a king? On the contrary, where is there a breach of faith or a transgression which has not been denounced by the law of God; and many are the instances of passages which were revealed to deter from the commission of evil acts and so frustrate unlawful designs. How different this from that!

And now another point. Both the cancelled passages and those which cancel remain equally in the text of the Coran. One can imagine an unhappy Moslem, upright and earnest, who morning and evening reads his Coran with humility and reverence, unable to distinguish between the commands that remain and those that have passed away, lost in bewilderment, giving vent to his anxiety in such thoughts as these: "Alas! why all this opposition and contradiction? Can these opposing passages

[1] Râzi and Sirat Al Nabueyata.

have proceeded from different sources? Nay, God forbid! for the Scripture hath been sent down from the One Almighty, and from Him alone. Then, whence such contrarieties, and where the key to my dilemma? Here are verses enjoining peace, tolerance, and free action as a perpetual obligation in the Faith (and he muses over such texts as those admonishing the Prophet that he is but a preacher and a warner, forbidden to use constraint and force, commissioned simply to deliver his message, whether they will hear or whether they will forbear:—'With thee is the message, with Us the account');—all this sent in compassion from the great God, just as spake Jesus and his holy apostles. What! can the High and Holy One turn back from His word; the All-wise and Merciful annul His command? Never; the Lord forbid! Had God sent His Prophet to fight against the heathen and compel them to enter the Faith, would He ever have revealed such texts as those forbidding force and couched in terms incapable of change? Could the Lord have commanded Jehâd, and He able under any contingency Himself to succour and exalt His messenger? Where is the way of escape, and which of these revelations shall I accept? I have been reading both one and the other all my life as equally my rule of faith and practice, and now I know not which are gone and which remain, which disannul and which are the disannulled. *Lâ houl, wa lâ —!*"

The embarrassment will be all the greater when he reflects on the challenge which he finds in the Coran itself: "If it had been from any other than God, they would have found therein many a discrepancy." His bewilderment, too, will be increased when he sees the doctors of Islam contending among themselves as to which passages cancel and which are cancelled, as if the great question were not whether there could in a divine revelation be discrepancy, contradiction, or cancelment at all; and yet (as we have seen in the first chapter) they spend their time in nothing but petty discussion of verbal differences and such like.[1] All that we ask, as the matter of supreme import, is, whether the cancelling verse is not in contradiction to the cancelled, and the text abrogated irreconcilable with that which abrogates it. And what, O Believer, dost thou call this discord and dissent? Perceivest thou not between the two sets of passages in this chapter an inapproachable divergence; and if in the Coran there are thus so many contradictions, from whom does the revelation come? We leave the answer to thy wise and impartial judgment. May the Lord guide thee aright; and to him that chooseth the right, He will grant a gracious reward.

[1] See pp. 23–26.

CHAPTER IV

ON PASSAGES IN THE CORAN TESTIFYING THAT THE TOURÂT AND THE GOSPEL HAVE NOT BEEN ALTERED, NOR SUFFERED VERBAL CORRUPTION

I. *Cloak not the truth with falsehood; nor conceal the truth while ye know it.*—SURA AL BACR (ii.) v. 39.

Commentary.—A command to depart from deception and error. The first clause refers to persons who bring in superfluous matters to confuse those who are listening to the evidences of the truth; and the second, to persons who withhold the truth altogether from those thus precluded from hearing it. "Clothe not," that is, envelope not, the truth in doubts suggested to the hearers; and that because the texts in the Tourât and Gospel regarding Mohammed embrace a hidden meaning which needs to be set forth: and those here referred to wrangled about those evidences, and suggested doubts to the mind of the inquirers.—*Razi.*

And *Beidhawi*: Clothe not the truth revealed unto you with false interpretations of your own, hiding it so that the one cannot be distinguished from the other; or do not disguise the truth by mingling it with the false, so as to hide it within its folds; or by false interpretations. "Hiding the truth as though they knew it"; commanded to abandon error, they misled those who heard, and hid the truth from such as did not hear it; knowing all the time they were doing wrong.

So also *Jelalein*, shortly: Mixing up the true with the false, and so changing it; knowingly hiding the truth in respect of the Prophet.

Remarks.—The leading Commentators are agreed

on the sense of the text: the "clothing" and "hiding" refer to the interpretation of passages and the withholding of them. Thus, according to the Coran, the People of the Book knew of passages bearing on the description and character of the Prophet, but did not dare, nor did their forefathers, to exclude or alter them. They simply denied that such passages when quoted bore evidence in favour of Mohammed; or they withheld their evidence altogether. The clear inference is, that they believed in their own Scriptures as a Revelation from God; and so the imputation made by some Moslems as to corruption of the text falls to the ground, and has no claim to our attention. It is quite clear that nothing more was imputed by Mohammed to the Jews than misinterpretation and withholding evidence.

11. *Do ye indeed desire that they (the Jews) should believe on you? and truly a part of them, when they had heard the word of God, perverted the same after they understood it, and they well knew.*—SURA BACR (ii.) v. 72.

Commentary.—Abstract of the most received interpretations—

It is said that the Prophet and his Companions desired that the Jews should embrace Islam, but they refused; on which the text was revealed. Others, however, think that it refers to their ancestors in the time of Moses. Imam Râzi takes the former view, as the pronoun evidently refers back to the Jews whom the Prophet desired to convert.

Authorities differ as to the meaning of the words "they perverted." The term (*tahrif*), it is held, implies either change of word or change of meaning, and some adopt the former, *i.e.* that the text was altered. But if that be not the case, then the "perversion" must be in the interpretation. We assume that the Tourât was revealed consecutively, as was the Coran, in perfect form. Now, if the changes were in the time of Moses, they would naturally have had no relation to matters bearing on the advent of Mohammed. The probability therefore is, that the "perversion" or change was made, not in the time of Moses, but in that of the Prophet, in such passages as related to his description and character; or it may have been that they made alterations in the law, as in the passage which enjoins stoning for adultery; but the Coran does not tell us what it was they changed. Some speak of the repetition of the same idea in the words "understood" and "knew," as mere surplusage; but it is not so; for (1) after they "understood" the word of God, they gave it a corrupt interpretation, while they "knew" it was contrary to the will of God; or (2) they "understood" the purport of God, and they "knew" that their evil interpretation would bring calamity and punishment from the Almighty.—*Râzi*.

Beidhawi: Some of them, that is, a party of their ancestors, heard the Torât and changed it,—*i.e.* such as the description of Mohammed, or the verse for stoning,—or the interpretation thereof, explaining passages according to their own desires. "After they understood it," *i.e.* had no doubt of the true meaning. And they "knew" the same, *i.e.* that they were fabricators and abrogators. The object of the text is this, that the Jewish Rabbis were no better than their ancestors; the Prophet, therefore, was not to rely on their folly and ignorance, for they would disbelieve and corrupt the word, as their fathers had done before them.

Remarks.—What has preceded in respect of the first text will suffice in respect of the absence of change in the Scripture. We shall not stop to make observations on each text as it occurs. It is only necessary here to note that both Beidhawi and Râzi agree as to *tahrîf* in this verse meaning not change in the text, but corrupt interpretation and concealment. But they differ as to the "party" here accused of the perversion; Râzi thinking that they belonged to the time of Mohammed, and Beidhawi to the age of Moses. It does not matter which.

The main point is, what *tahríf* really consisted in, *i.e.* in the interpretation or concealment, as in the holding back of the text on the question of stoning —not its alteration. The idea of "the change of words from their places," or the possibility of such change in the transmission of the Scripture, will be amply shown to be groundless in what is to follow.

III. *When a prophet came unto them from God attesting that (Scripture) which is with them, a part of those to whom the Book was given cast the Book of God behind their backs, as if they knew not.*—SURA BACR (ii.) v. 97.

Commentary.—That which was "cast away" was the Tourât; and if it be asked how that consists with their being said to "hold by" the same, we answer, that as the Tourât bore witness to the description and person of the Prophet, such as made obligatory the acceptance of the Faith, their rejection of Islam was equivalent to casting the Tourât aside. "As if they knew not," signifying that it was done with due knowledge of the truth. The text also proves that they were aware of the truth of the Prophet's mission, seeing that they opposed that which they knew.—*Râzi.*

Jelalein: "Cast it away"; *i.e.* they acted in respect of the testimony of the Tourât to the Prophet, etc., as if they knew not that he was the true Prophet, and it the Book of God.

Remarks.—The reader will see, thank God! that every passage quoted in this chapter decisively supports all that has preceded in respect of the integrity of "the Book." No intelligent person but must observe that the "casting of their Scriptures behind their backs," means disobedience in not accepting the proofs of Mohammed's mission held to be in the Tourât, and opposing that in it which they knew to be true; not the putting out any part of it. But while Mohammed clearly maintained that the Jews possessed their Book untampered with, he at the same time accused them of misinterpretation, hiding, and "casting away"; that is, of suggesting doubts, suppressing evidence, and shutting their eyes to the testimony borne by these Scriptures to his mission: all which should show to the believers in the Coran that the Old Testament Scriptures are accredited by Mohammed as free from the taint of corruption.

IV. *Verily they that hide that which God hath sent down of the Book, and sell the same for a small price, they shall consume only fire in their bellies; God shall not speak with them in the Day of Resurrection, nor purify them, and they shall suffer a grievous punishment.*—SURA BACR (ii.) v. 170.

Commentary.—Ibn Abbas tells us that this text was revealed in respect of Kab ibn Ashraf and other leading Jews, who were in the habit of receiving offerings from their followers. When the Prophet appeared, they feared the loss of these gifts, and so they concealed the prophecies regarding him and his dispensation; he also considers that the "hiding" consisted in altering (يحرفون) the Tourât and the Gospel. But this cannot be accepted by the learned, for both Tourât and Gospel had been handed down in widespread and unbroken succession, which rendered that out of the question. The meaning, then, was, that they kept back the true interpretation of passages well known amongst them to bear on the mission of the Prophet, and introduced false explanations which diverted their true meaning as revealed by God, or, in other words, hid it.—*Râzi*.

Jelalein: "For a small price," that is, for revenues received from their followers, and fear of their loss: their drink would be the Fire.

Remarks.—Note, first, the admission of the learned Doctors, that tampering with the Tourât and Gospel was impossible, because of the widespread and unbroken succession of the Jewish and Christian Scriptures throughout the world. Change in the text is here admitted to be out of the question. Note, secondly, that "hiding" means concealment of the true sense of passages in the Book by false glosses, diverting them thus from their true significance. Now these two points are unequivocal evidence, not only that the People of the Book never dared to tamper with the text of their Scripture, but that they were its trusted custodians, even as it was originally revealed to them. Further, if the Jewish chiefs did, as we are told, so "hide" the testimony of their Scripture relating to Mohammed, from the fear of losing influence in the eyes of their people, and also the support they had hitherto enjoyed, it follows that they did so either by the misinterpretation imputed to them in the preceding verses, or by keeping back passages, as is supposed in the present text and the commentary thereon. And if the learned Doctors of Islam in after days held this view, how much more did the Prophet himself believe in the integrity and purity of the Scriptures, who said: "O ye People of the Book, why do ye deny the revelation of God, to which ye yourselves bear witness"; that is, feign ignorance before those who have never heard it, while all the time ye know the same, and bear witness to it?

V. *O ye People of the Book, why do ye deny the*

revelation of God, and yet ye are witnesses of the same?
—Sura Al Imrân (iii.) v. 68.

Commentary.—(1) The revelation (or "verses") here spoken of means the Tourât and Gospel, which foretell of Mohammed. (2) The Jews are accused as deniers of the very essence of the Tourât, seeing that they altered the same, and belied the existence of the passages which bore evidence of the Prophet's mission. "And ye bear witness," meaning that in presence of the Moslems and their own people they denied the existence of such passages in the Tourât and Gospel; then, when they were alone with certain of themselves, they admitted their existence; just like the text, "Ye seek to make it crooked, and yet ye are witnesses thereof" (Sura Baer, v. 99).—*Râzi.*

Remarks.—From this verse and the commentary, we gather that the Jews did not remove from their Scriptures the passages which, as Mohammed supposed, bore testimony to his person and mission. The text is equally clear against any tampering with the Scriptures, for they are said to have denied the existence of such passages in them, while yet (when alone) they admitted their being there; and this leaves no place whatever for the imputation that they tampered with their Book. If there had been any desire so to do, their first temptation would have been to remove such passages altogether from their Book, fearing their evidence in favour of Mohammed, or to have altered them, instead of simply disbelieving or withholding their testimony, "while they yet bore witness to them," as parts of their Scripture. And as they did not do anything of the kind, it follows that they bestowed diligent and devoted care in maintaining their Scripture intact as it was revealed to them by the Most High.

VI. *Verily, there is amongst them a party that change their tongues in (reading) the Book, that ye might think it to be from the Book, and it is not from the Book. And they say, " This is from God," yet it is not from God; and they utter a lie against God, knowing all the while.*—SURA IMRÂN (iii.) v. 77.

Commentary.—The Jews are said to have "altered" their tongues, *i.e.* to have asserted a thing and then contradicted it, and so given a tortuous meaning. Others explain it as changing (*tahríf*) of words, as the Arabs used to do in some of their dubious expressions. And if it be asked how could there be change (*tahríf*) in the Tourât, spread as it was universally all over the world, the answer is, that perhaps it was practised only by a few, who passed off their manipulated matter on some of the people, and on such a supposition *tahríf* might have been possible.

Râzi, on the other hand (speaking for himself), says that to him the most reasonable interpretation is, that as the passages referred to bore on the prophetical office of Mohammed, they therefore needed for their explanation close inquiry and inward thought; and here the Jews introduced misleading points and faithless objections, so as to cast doubt on their evidence for Islam in the minds of those that listened; for the Jews would hold that the meaning of God in revealing these verses was that which we say, not what you say; and that is the real meaning of *tahríf*, and "changing the tongue," or perversion in speech. In fact, it is just what we see in our own day, when passages are quoted from the Word of God, and the captious disputant introduces questions and doubts, saying that this is not the Lord's meaning, but so and so.—*Râzi.*

And *Jelalein*: A party of the People of the Book, as Kab ibn Ashraf, "change with their tongues"; *i.e.* in their reading of the Book they join passages with others out of their places, thus changing the meaning (*tahríf*) in respect of the description of the Prophet, "that ye may think it," *i.e.* the perverted passage, to be from God; and it is not so. And they repeat against God a lie, "they well knowing" that they are liars.

Remarks.—This is a text which is so clear as hardly to need comment. It resembles those preceding it, and shows clearly what the perversion (*tahríf*) of the Tourât charged against the Jews really was, that is, reciting passages in such a way as to give them a wrong meaning. They "knew that they were speaking a lie against God," *i.e.* something opposed to the text of their Tourât,—a clear proof that they dared not tamper with the text itself.

Now I praise the Imâm Râzi, and admire his fairness, in that he has not allowed himself to be drawn into the path of those shallow thinkers who, when asked how changes could have been made in the Scripture, gave so weak and silly an answer. They say, "*perhaps* a small party may have done it, and then passed off the manipulated matter on others of their people." But the very word "perhaps" shows that it was felt to be no real argument at all; and how could "a small party" have tampered with the Tourât? Let them tell us, if they can, how it would have been possible from the very beginning. Are they so ignorant of the history of the Beni Israel, that there were vast multitudes under the leadership of Moses before the Law was revealed; that it was read to his people during his lifetime for forty years; that after him followed Joshua and a succession of prophets, all acquainted with the Scriptures; and then, long before the rise of Islam, that these were spread abroad everywhere in such abundance as to render any change impossible? How, then, does the "perhaps" fall into an impossibility!

And, after all, the interpretation of these Commentators is quite sufficient for our purpose, since they hold that the party thus referred to falsified the passages "*with their tongues*"; they did not touch the texts themselves, or remove them from the Tourât, simply made the meaning doubtful to the hearers by equivocal suggestions and fallacious arguments. So that, even in their view, this, and no more, is meant by *tahrîf* and change (لي) with their tongues. And therein is matter for reflection.

VII. *And when God took the covenant of those to whom the Book was given,—" That ye shall publish it to mankind, and shall not hide it"; yet they cast it behind their backs, and sold it for a small price. Wretched is that which they sold it for.*—SURA AL IMRÂN (iii.) v. 185.

Commentary.—The followers of Moses and Jesus, to injure the Prophet, concealed the passages in the Tourât and Gospel bearing on his mission; and tampered (*tahrîf*) with them, or placed false interpretations on them and suggested unworthy doubts.—*Râzi.*

And *Jelalein*: The Jews acted so "for a small gain," namely, the being looked up to by their followers as learned authorities; and they hid these passages for fear of losing that position: a miserable bargain!

Remarks.—We have no instance anywhere of Mohammed casting reflection on the safe guardianship of the Tourât and Gospel; and he always speaks of the Jews and Christians as "the People of the Book"; neither does he ever throw out any suspicion that the Tourât, as in their hands, was any other than "the Book" revealed to Moses, nor the Gospel other than that revealed to Jesus (as some ignorant Moslems of the present day talk); he simply accuses them of confusing and hiding the evidence which (as he claimed) bore testimony to himself; just as the Imam has told us before, they brought misleading and embarrassing questions to bear on passages that required careful thought and nice discrimination.

From all this we conclude, first, that no Moslem is justified in imputing *tahríf*, in the sense of *tampering with the text*, to the People of the Book; and second, that every Moslem is bound to look reverently on the Tourât and Gospel as now in the hands of Jews and Christians; and himself to search therein for the proofs they were asserted to contain of the mission of their Prophet; and not only so, but he is bound to accept all that is contained in them, and to be guided himself thereby.

VIII. *Of the Jews there are that change the word from its place, and who say,* " *We have heard, and have disobeyed*"; *and* "*hear without being made to hear*"; *and* "*Râina*" (look on us), *changing* (*the sense*) *with their tongues, and speaking evil of the faith. Now, if they had said,* " *We have heard and have obeyed,*" *and* " *Hearken and behold us,*" *it had been better for them, and more upright. But God hath cursed them for their unbelief, and they shall not believe excepting a few.*—SURA AL NISA (iii.) v. 44.

Commentary.— Some explain it thus: the Jews changed (*tahríf*) one word for another, as ربعة (*middle stature*) into آدم طويل (*Adam lofty in stature*); and if it be asked how this could be, seeing that the Scripture, in word and letter, had been regularly handed down, and spread all the world over, to the east and to the west, we answer, first, that possibly it may have been when the people, and especially those versed in the Book, were few in number, and so the change was possible. And, secondly, the meaning of *tahrîf* is the casting of vain doubts on passages in the Tourât; just as schismatics in our own day do in respect of passages in the Coran adverse to their tenets; and this is the true interpretation. It is also said that the Jews used to come and ask the Prophet some question, and when he had answered, they would go forth and change (*tahrîf*) his words.—*Râzi*.

And *Jelalein*: They "changed the word from its place," *i.e.* in which God had placed it; or its critical mark; or altered its position, so as to give it another meaning from that originally intended.

IX. *They change the word from its place.*—SURA AL MAIDA (V.) v. 14.

Commentary.—That is, they change (*tahrîf*) the word from the position in which God had placed it; meaning commands, sanctions, and prohibitions, as laid down in His Word. The Commentators cite in point the well-known case of the adulterers of Kheibar. Now the penalty in the Tourât is stoning. But the Jews, looking to the rank of the offenders, sent a deputation to the Prophet, hoping he would order a lighter punishment, saying at the same time to them, "If he order stoning, beware, and do not consent." When they had put the question to Mohammed, Gabriel brought down the command for stoning. So they refused the judgment; on which Gabriel desired the Prophet to propose Ibn Sûreya of Fadak as arbiter between them. When Mohammed had named him and described his person to them, they said he was the best versed in the Scriptures of any Jew on the whole face of the earth, and were content that he should judge. So the Prophet put Ibn Sûreya on his solemn oath as to whether the punishment for adultery was stoning in the Tourât. He replied that it was; whereupon the Jewish rabble leapt upon him; but he was firm, saying that he feared to tell a lie for the punishment thereof. Thereupon the Prophet ordered both offenders to be stoned to death at the gate of the Mosque. And so the text about "changing the word from its place" refers to this affair, and to the substitution of "scourging," in place of "stoning to death."

Remarks.—These two verses tell the same thing. Three interpretations are given: (1) change of one word for another; (2) wrong exposition; (3) suppression. The first has been sufficiently disposed of;[1] just one point is new, viz. the alleged difference as to the height of our father Adam. One marvels at such vain objections; for where do we find in the Tourât that Adam was tall in stature? A mere hallucination of some foolish creature seized on as *tahrîf*! It had become the critics better to have searched the pages of the Tourât, and not to have fallen into this slough. Praise be to the Lord that this solitary instance of alleged verbal alteration (*tahrîf*) so utterly falls to the ground! And what is most surprising of all is, the failure of the Commentators to notice the bearing of those passages of the Coran, in which the Jews are said to have admitted the existence of verses in their books, which texts are said to have given evidence of Mohammed's mission, but were clothed by them in a false dress; which simply means that they interpreted them otherwise, or concealed them; so that no room whatever is left for the imputation of *tahrîf*, or textual change, at any period, either in early or later times. If, indeed, there had been suspicion of textual interpolation, it would certainly have been mentioned in the Coran, as well as misinterpretation and concealment. But the Commentators themselves have no faith in any such imputation, since they qualify the suggestion, even when they make it, with the proviso "possibly," showing

---

[1] See pp. 85, 86.

that, after all their endeavours, the conjecture is of the weakest and shallowest nature. We need not, however, press the point further, since the Imâm himself, and others of the same high stamp, attach no credit whatever to it, as we have already seen.

"Change of the word from its place" is said to signify false glosses, or suppression, as in the case of the Kheibar adulterers; or perversion by his visitors of Mohammed's own words, as mentioned in the Imam's note on the first verse.[1]

X. *And how shall they make thee their judge, since they already have the Tourât, in which is the judgment of God? then they will turn their backs after that, and they are not true believers.*—SURA AL MAIDA (v.) v. 44.

Commentary.—An expression of surprise from the Almighty at the Jews appealing to the Prophet in the case of the adulterer, while they had already the punishment of stoning laid down in their Tourât. This was evidence of their obstinacy and falsity, in that they turned aside from the command of God in their Scripture, and sought exemption from Mohammed to give up the practice of stoning for adultery; and consented to an appeal from the Word of God to the word of one (Ibn Sûreya) in whose admission even they had no faith.—*Râzi.*

And *Jelalein*: "How shall they make thee their judge," and they already have the sentence for stoning? They were not seeking after the truth, but for what was the easiest for them. "Turned their backs," that is, from the command which they knew to be in their Scriptures. Then follows: "We have sent down the Tourât, in which is guidance and light," that is, guidance from error, and a knowledge of the commandments.

Remarks.—Three important conclusions from this

[1] See p. 89.

verse as commented on:—First, the testimony that the Tourât, as in the hands of the Jews, contained the law of God, which sets at rest any question of *tahrîf* in the sense of tampering; for every intelligent Moslem must see that if there had been textual corruption, there would have been nothing authoritative to refer to; and here we are told of the Jews that "they had the Tourât, in which is the judgment (commandment or law) of God." Second, it follows that the Tourât was sufficient for their guidance, apart from the word of Mohammed or any other; since it sufficed (as we are told) in the case of adultery; and so in every other matter, for it is described as "a guide out of the ways of error." Third, as the Jews are said to have applied to the Prophet in the hope of obtaining from him a sentence "easier for them than the law of the Tourât," it follows that they did not dare to tamper with their Scripture in order to obtain the relaxation of their law which they desired; and even if they had so desired, any such tampering would have been impossible, owing to the universal spread of their Scriptures all over the world. "With them," that is, "in their hands, is the Tourât." Consider this: The Tourât, in which are the commands of God, is here affirmed to be in use by the Jews; the Scripture which, as shown above, is genuine and free from touch. Let the candid believer lay it to heart.

XI. *And let the People of the Gospel judge according to that which is revealed therein; and whoso judgeth not according to that which God hath revealed, these are the wicked ones.*—SURA AL MAIDA (V.) v. 48.

Commentary.—If it be asked how the Gospel could have been the rule of judgment after the appearance of the Coran, we reply: (1) that the Christians were bound to accept the evidences revealed in their Gospel as to the mission of Mohammed; there can be no doubt about this; (2) that they should still follow whatever in the Gospel is not abrogated by the Coran; (3) they are warned against tampering with their Scriptures, like the Jews who suppressed the commands of the Tourât. "That the people of the Gospel may judge," etc.; that is, let them study the Gospel as God has revealed it, without *tahrif* or change.—*Rázi.*

Remarks.—It will not have escaped my good reader that the testimony here given of the integrity of the Gospel in the days of Mohammed, and of its freedom from any change, is clear, seeing that Christians are exhorted to abide by the commands which God has revealed therein. The comment that this means the evidence of Mohammed's mission, is but a testimony to the integrity of the Gospel; for if it had been tampered with, what would have been the use of referring them to its testimony? And the same inference arises from the other interpretation of the text, as warning the Christians to avoid the example of the Jews in perverting and hiding the commandments of the Tourât.

Two clear and important lessons follow from this verse: (1) the integrity of the New Testament as absolutely free from imputation of *tahrif* or change; (2) the obligation devolving upon the followers of Mohammed, equally with the People of the Gospel, to be guided by all that is revealed therein, not merely in respect of its alleged support of the mission of Mohammed, but also in respect of its testimony to Jesus Christ. Since, after the evidence that has been given (and what is to follow) of the authenticity and purity of the Gospel, it is not open to the Moslem to accept parts of it and refuse others; he is bound to accept *the whole*, as a guide of life and faith revealed from above.

XII. *The similitude of those who have been charged with the burden of the Tourât and have not borne it, is as the similitude of the Ass laden with books. Wretched is the similitude of that people. They give the lie to the religion of God, and God guideth not the transgressing people.*—SURA AL JAMAA (lxii.) v. 5.

Commentary.—" Laden with the Tourât," that is, charged to act in accordance with it, which the Jews failed to do, neglecting the intimation of the Prophet's advent, like an ass laden with books and none the better for it. Evil is the similitude of those who give the lie to prophecies of the kind.—*Jelalein.*

And *Râzi*: Such is the similitude given by the Almighty of those who, having this revelation, fail to act in accordance with its precepts. They are like the ass; for they are as little benefited. The Tourât gives the description of Mohammed, with good tidings of his coming and of his faith. They were "given this Tourât to carry," that is, to give effect to its instructions and take their stand thereon; and failing to do this and believe on the Prophet, they resembled the ass which, laden with books, was unaware of their contents; or as one who, knowing the teaching of the Coran, lives as if he had no need of it.

Remarks.—The text is evidence that the Jews of the day believed in the Tourât, as their fathers had done before them, and faithfully preserved it as by Moses handed down. The metaphor of the ass is clear as to the absence of any tampering with their books, for the ass does nothing of the sort, nor can. In like manner, the Jews did nothing to injure the text, only they ignored its testimony in favour of Mohammed, and failed to act in accordance with its precepts. The Tourât being thus accredited, and the text continuing as it then was up to the present day, and being available to all in Arabic as the counterpart of the Hebrew, why do our Moslem friends not set themselves now to its perusal, searching in its prophecies and types for the intimations alleged to be there in respect of their Prophet? Let them do so, and they will find none. To the fair and unprejudiced student, the notices it contains are as far from Islam as the heavens from the earth.

But how vastly are we not indebted to the Coran for the testimony it gives us of the safe custody and preservation of both Tourât and Gospel; not, indeed, as if we ourselves, being People of the Book, stood in need of any such testimony, but we earnestly long that the Moslem world should enjoy the light of its blessed teaching, and, sharing our joy, may believe in it as the Word which God hath revealed for our salvation.

XIII. *They to whom WE have given the Book recognise him as they recognise their own sons; they that injure their own souls, these will not believe.*—SURA INAM, Meccan, (vi.) v. 20.

Commentary.—Whence was this recognition of the Prophet, as of their own sons, to be derived? First, it may be said, that the Tourât and the Gospel contained predictions that a Prophet was to arise in the latter time, and call the world to the true faith. Or, secondly, that, in addition, detailed intimation was given of the time and place at which he was to appear, of his descent, stature, appearance, etc. Now as to the first, such indefinite prediction would have been insufficient to indicate the person of the Prophet, and enable them to recognise him as they did their own sons. The second explanation, again, would imply that every Jew and Christian must everywhere have at once recognised Mohammed from the description so given, and the idea of falsehood on so vast a scale is not admissible; for we know of a certainty that the Tourât and Gospel did not contain any such particulars as would have sufficed for the purpose. If it be objected (1) that particulars of this nature may have existed at the time the Prophet arose; or (2) that they originally existed, but had been already tampered with and left out at some previous period;—the reply to the first is, that the concealment of such detailed predictions would have been impossible, seeing that the Scriptures said to contain them were spread over the whole world; and the second is equally out of the question, as in that case there would not have been Jew or Christian in any land, at the rise of Islam, possessing any knowledge of the promised coming of the Prophet; so that this too falls to the ground.

The real purport of the text is, that Jews and Christians versed in their Scriptures, and thus men of discernment and judgment, were able to test the evidence of Mohammed's mission, and to estimate the weight of his miracles, and consequently to recognise him as sent by God; and the metaphor in the text as to this recognition is thus quite in point.

Remarks.—The Imâm has done well to admit the impossibility of the Tourât and Gospel containing any detailed prediction of the time, place, appearance, etc., of the coming Prophet; and so the idea that the People of the Book could not help recognising him falls thus to the ground. His own interpretation implies (1) that the Jews and Christians were "men of discernment and judgment"; (2) that they were witnesses of the Prophet's miracles; and (3) that they consequently recognised him as sent of God. On the first, I observe that the People of the Book being in Mohammed's time men of discernment and intelligence, contradicts the previous text likening them to the ass; and again, how could they have recognised him from their Scriptures as the coming Prophet if they were as ignorant of the testimony they contained as the ass is ignorant of what is in the load of books upon its back? Could any contradiction be greater than this? Which of the two passages are we to receive? Again, if the People of the Book, possessing intelligence and judgment in respect of their Scriptures, yet found no evidence therein regarding Mohammed, it follows that they could not have recognised him to be the coming Prophet "as they recognised their own sons"; for where is the man that recognises his son and then denies him, but one that is lost to all sense of humanity?

On the second point, how can it be said that the People of the Book should have been convinced by the miracles of Mohammed, since, as we saw in the first chapter, he wrought no miracle? Alas, that the Imám should have played here so childish a part, and avoided an argument which can carry no weight with any one having the least acquaintance with the Moslem faith! And his third point fails with the second; for if they saw no miracle, they could not therefrom have believed in the prophetic mission of Mohammed. So that the idea of the Jews knowing him as they knew their own sons, must have been either a mere conjecture, or based on the saying of some of the Jewish converts. Thus of Abdallah ibn

Salam it is said that, meeting Omar, he told him that he recognised Mohammed as the Prophet of God more surely than he recognised his own son, for of the legitimacy of the latter he never could be so absolutely certain. Whereupon Omar arose and kissed him between his eyes; which shows that such was not by any means the confession of his people generally, even if converts to Islam.

Lastly, the text about the recognition of sons is an inestimable testimony to the Moslem of the faithful manner in which the People of the Book have watched over its integrity. The Imâm, as we have seen, has gone in his questions by way of exact analysis into the inability of the People of the Book to recognise the Prophet as they did their own sons, and the impossibility of their having tampered with their Scriptures; and his reasoning is clear and irrefragable. Seeking to find an escape from the difficulty, he is landed in a conclusion which not only does not in the least help him, but actually proves the absurdity of the statement that the Jews recognised the Prophet in Mohammed as they recognised their own sons. So that the Imâm rather criticises than substantiates the text.

XIV. *And if thou art in doubt as to that which WE have revealed unto thee, ask those who read the Book (revealed) before thee, for verily the truth hath come unto thee from thy Lord. Be not thou, therefore, among those who doubt.*—SURA YUNAS (x.) v. 92.

Commentary (abridged).—Some hold that it is the Prophet in his own person who is here addressed; others, that it is some other party; others, again, that it is the Prophet, but only so in appearance, as in the Arabic proverb, in which, by "thee,"[1] some one else is meant. These last expositors think the text was addressed, not to Believers or Unbelievers, but to such as halted between two opinions, much in this sort of way: "O man, if thou art in doubt as to that which WE have revealed unto thee for guidance by the tongue of the Prophet, then ask the People of the Book, that they may assure thee of the truth of his mission."

There is difference of opinion also as to who the People of the Book are to whom reference is here desired to be made. The best opinion is, that they were Jews who had come over to Islam, as the two Kabs, Abdallah, etc. Others hold that it means both those who had become Moslems and those who had not. And if it be asked by such as hold that the Scriptures were tampered with, how confidence could still be placed in those same Scriptures, we reply that the tampering consisted in the hiding of such passages as bore testimony to Mohammed; and if, nevertheless, there remained in them that which proved the mission, the appeal becomes all the stronger.

Lastly, if we suppose the Prophet himself to be here addressed in his own person as "thou," the explanation is that, being a man, he was, as such, liable to be troubled in his heart by doubts and anxious possibilities, which could only be removed by clear declarations and manifest proofs; and the Almighty therefore made this revelation to dispel these misgivings. And after all, it is only stated as a possibility, "*if*" thou art in doubt. (The above from *Kâzi*.)

And *Beidhawi*: "The People of the Book have clear evidence in their Scriptures of the truth of their history, in the manner that WE have made known their story unto thee"; the reference being to the truth thereof, and the testimony borne to it in the preceding revelation. The Prophet is referred to the People of the Book as well versed in the veracity of its contents; or, it is a stirring up of the Prophet, and consolidation of evidence, that there should be no possibility of doubt in his mind.

Also *Jelalein*: "If thou, O Prophet, art in doubt as to that which WE have revealed unto thee of past histories, ask those who read the Book revealed before thee, for it is steadfastly believed in by them, and they will assure thee of the truth thereof."

آياك اعنى واسمعي يا جاره

Remarks.—The learned Doctors are sadly embarrassed by this verse. Referring the Prophet, as it does, to the People of the Book who would solve his doubts, they have striven to explain it in such a way as might maintain his dignity, and are thus driven to interpretations, the strangest one has ever heard, such as that it is addressed ostensibly to the Prophet, but really to such as questioned his claim,—which is in the last degree opposed to the sense of the text. Others admit that it was Mohammed himself that is addressed; but, however much they change and turn the compass, it ever points to the same celestial pole, —the purity and preservation of the Scriptures. If, again, we take the party addressed to be those who doubted the truth of Islam, this throws open the whole foundation of the Prophet's mission, regarding which these are referred to the Jews for an answer to their doubts; which would only strengthen the argument for the authority of the Scriptures,—a result the Moslem critics will hardly be prepared for.

Now, if the person addressed be the Prophet himself (the more received and natural view), the appeal is conclusive as to the faithful guardianship of their Scriptures by the Jews; for when doubt of his mission, and distracting questionings as to what "WE have revealed to thee," arose in his heart, he is referred to them,—"Ask those who read the Book revealed before thee"; and thus his doubts would be dispelled and set at rest by the evidence and light of their Scriptures. This is so clear a testimony to their authenticity that it leaves no room for the

Imâm's question (p. 99,—" If it be asked by those who hold the Scriptures tampered with, how confidence could still be placed in them," etc.). How could the Imâm treat the text in this cold and indifferent manner, as if it admitted any doubt; for if the Book had been corrupted, what confidence could have been placed therein, or the Prophet have been referred to it to calm and remove his misgivings? It was unworthy of the Imâm to play thus fast and loose. Had he forgotten the proofs he himself had given in this chapter, that no imputation of tampering could hold good, and that *tahrîf* was nothing more than "hiding," "misinterpretation," or "changing with the tongue" words away from their proper meaning? And, indeed, had there been no other testimony than this present verse, it would have been a decisive answer to anyone who would impeach the integrity of the Book, and the faithful custody of its possessors. The idea of the party addressed being Jewish converts to Islam is clearly inadmissible, as we learn from the comments, and from the preceding verse. So also with the suggestions of Beidhawi and Jelalein, that the doubts in the Prophet's mind related to the historical notices in the Tourât; for what possible connection could the text have had with these?

Kâzi hits the nail on the head. The doubts and questionings were, as he says, in the Prophet's own heart. And when he was commanded to refer to the People of the Book for reassurance, it equally results that his followers are bound to ascertain in like manner the testimony of the preceding Scriptures, and accept their decision in all matters of faith and doctrine, and the line dividing the true from the false. Where, then, is the talk about *tahríf*, as if it meant tampering with the text! The testimony of the Coran should satisfy every honest Moslem of the safe guardianship of the People of the Book, and consequent purity and authority of the Holy Scriptures.

REVIEW

The foregoing passages of the Coran, with the explanations of the most famous and reliable Doctors of Islam, prove incontestably the integrity of the Tourât and Gospel. Anyone talking of *tahríf* or corruption, contradicts the Coran, and denies the evidence of what is held a direct revelation from Heaven. He who impeaches "the Book" impeaches the Coran, and is not worthy to be called a Believer, for he casts the Coran behind his back.

And now, O Moslem! dost thou satisfy thy soul by lip-service to the Coran, without reflection on its meaning; or read its teaching, and yet not act upon it? Thou sayest, "Nay, but I do reflect, and also act." Then it behoves thee to believe the Tourât and Gospel,—the "Book" attested thus by the Coran as genuine and authentic, and (the Coran being witness) beyond the breath of change. Take and read it, as thy bounden duty, at eventide and in the morning; learn its testimony, and lay to heart its precepts;—a Book from which the Coran derived its ancient chronicles and knowledge. And dost thou not perceive that the Coran itself is none other than a guide that, by bearing testimony to the Scriptures, would lead thee to their perusal, and obedience to their precepts? Abounding, as it does, with histories of the past, it, as it were, invites to search the original from whence those histories were derived; just as if one passed a friend whose hands were filled with rare and precious gems, found in a mine hard by, would he not at once go on to that mine and gather for himself specimens of the rich material; or if, shutting his eyes, he turned therefrom, would it not be regarded as foolishness and stupidity? And here is this precious treasure at thy very door.

The Christian advocate, indeed, need hardly waste his strength in proving to Mussulmans the genuineness of "the Book," for the proof lies in the Coran itself, as attested by the learned of their own faith. Believers in the Coran have no need, therefore, for testimony from without. And if they believe in that testimony of the Coran as to the divine authority of those Scriptures, as they certainly would have believed it had they lived in the days of their Prophet, does it not follow that they should devote themselves to their study now, accept what they reveal, and reject all else beside?

CHAPTER V

PASSAGES FROM THE CORAN SHOWING THAT PROPHECY AND REVELATION BELONG TO THE BENI ISRAEL

1. *O Children of Israel! Remember the favour wherewith I have favoured you and preferred you above all nations* (or *all creatures*).—SURA BACR (ii.) v. 44.

Commentary.—The Lord calls to mind His former benefits to the Children of Israel as a reason why they should not now refuse to obey His prophet. "Favoured you above all creatures" might be held to mean, "even above Mohammed," but that would be out of the question. (1) Some say the words imply simply a great multitude, as we speak of "a world of people"; but the word العلمين signifies every existing being beside the Creator; so that cannot stand. (2) Others, that "the whole world existing at the time being" is meant, not in the future; and so that would take Mohammed out of the comparison. (3) They were superior, others say, to all creatures; but only in one thing, that is, in the favour bestowed upon them, not in anything else.

Again, it is said that the "favour" conferred was only on the believing part of the nation, the rebellious being turned into apes and swine, and cursed of God. Nor is there anything to show that the same favour, whether in secular or spiritual things, would be continued, whether in this world or in that to come, otherwise why the solemn warning that follows: "Fear the day on which one soul shall be unable to make satisfaction for another"; the answer being, that rebellion, after great favour, is all the worse and more to be condemned; and hence the warning.—*Râzi.*

And *Jelalein*: Remember with thankfulness and obedience the favour wherewith I have favoured you, that is, your forefathers, beyond all the world of their time.

Remarks.—One has no objection to the interpretation, that the superiority here affirmed of the children of Israel simply means superiority over the rest of the world for the time being, except the conclusion that this must not be held to imply that they were preferred before Mohammed; and that for two reasons. (1) Supposing Mohammed to be the Prince of all the Prophets,— for whom, as they say, the heavens and the earth were created,—then the seed of Ishmael must certainly have been preferred over the seed of Israel (Jacob) as the more favoured race. If a prophet was to arise of the seed of Ishmael greater than any prophet of the seed of Israel, how then could it have been said that "WE have favoured" the latter beyond all the world, including at the moment the seed of Ishmael? The Almighty, to whom the end is as the beginning, must have known that this the greatest of all prophets was to be of the seed of Ishmael, and therefore that the seed of Ishmael (not that of Jacob) was the most favoured race of all the world, which would be in direct opposition to the present text. (2) We are told that Mohammed was the beginning of the creation; that he was a "*light*" which descended from the loins of father to son,—from Adam downwards,—till at the last the Prophet was born of Abdallah and Amina. In this descent, it is held, he was ever present in the world; and so it follows from this verse that the Almighty favoured the seed of Jacob over "the light" of Mohammed, which was at that moment in the loins of his ancestor of the day.

11. *And WE gave to him (Abraham) Isaac and Jacob, and both of them WE directed aright.*

Commentary.—If it be asked why only Isaac and Jacob are named as given by God to Abraham, and not also Ishmael, whose name is kept back till after the names of several others, we answer, that the object here is to mention the prophetical race of the Children of Israel, which altogether descended from Isaac and Jacob; while from Ishmael there descended no prophet but Mohammed alone. It was not therefore permissible to mention Mohammed in this place, since the Lord sent him to put down polytheism among the Arabs; while Abraham, in abandoning polytheism and taking hold of the unity, obtained great blessing both in spiritual and secular things,—his progeny becoming prophets and royal personages. Such being the case, Mohammed was barred from making mention of himself in that connection; and for the same reason from naming Ishmael along with Isaac.—*Râzi.*

Remarks.—The Imâm is here like one who, finding no outlet, and unable to scale the walls around him, retires discomfited. Observe that the question put is, Why Ishmael is not mentioned with Isaac and Jacob, but among other names in quite another connection? and the attempted explanation throws no light upon it, as you will see, for two reasons. First, the inquirer does not ask why *Mohammed* is not named with Moses and other prophets at the end of the verse, but why *Ishmael* is not mentioned along with Isaac; where, then, is the pertinence of the answer, "It was not therefore permissible to mention Mohammed in this place"? And how did the Imâm learn that the object of Isaac and Jacob—"the gift of God to Abraham"—being named here, was that from them descended the long line of Israelitish prophets? Supposing, however, that really to have been the reason, then why was their brother Ishmael not also named along with them, seeing that the greatest of all the prophets was (as the Imâm tells us) to arise from amongst the descendants of Ishmael? Second, if, according to the Imâm, the object in naming Isaac and Jacob as having been "directed aright" was to indicate the progeny of Abraham from whose line prophets should arise, then it follows from the absence of Ishmael's name that no prophet would arise from amongst his descendants; a point to be observed. And for the same reason the Imâm's remark about Mohammed being "barred from naming himself," falls to the ground, since he does not hold that the mention of Ishmael with Isaac has any reference to Mohammed. And so we see that aberration and disappointment have led to the invention of reasons that are utterly untenable.

III. *And when he (Abraham) had separated himself from them, and from that which they worshipped beside God, WE gave him Isaac and Jacob; and WE made them both prophets; and WE granted unto them (benefits of) our mercy; and WE granted unto them a lofty tongue of truth.*—SURA MARYAM (xix.) v. 49.

Commentary. When Abraham left his people, and gave up their faith and home, and went forth whither God had called him to go, the Lord gave him a son and grandson, both prophets, good gifts both for this life and the next; and of His mercy He furthermore granted them wealth and honour, and a pure and holy seed. He gave them also a true and noble tongue; blessings of the lips as well as blessings of the hand; according to the prayer of Abraham, "Grant unto me a tongue of truth among the race to come," so that he became a pattern of righteousness to all the religions of the world.—*Râzi*.

So also *Beidhawi*: Isaac and Jacob, God's gift to Abraham, are alone here mentioned as the root and ancestry from which the race of prophets sprang; or because it was the object to notice Ishmael in his excellence by himself. "And made them prophets," *i.e.* both of them, or from amongst them.

And *Jelalein*: When Abraham departed to the holy land, WE gave him a son and grandson to live with him, and made both prophets, and gave to them (*i.e.* to all three) of Our mercy, wealth, and children, and an exalted name among all religions.

IV. *And WE gave him Isaac and Jacob; and WE placed among his descendants the gift of prophecy and the Scriptures; and WE gave him his reward in this world, and in that to come he shall be one of the righteous.*—SURA AL ANKÁBÛT (xxix.) v. 25.

Commentary.—After explaining the verse, Râzi raises two questions. *First*, Ishmael was one of Abraham's children; why, then, is he not mentioned as well as Isaac and Jacob? The answer is, that he is included among the descendants "to whom WE granted the gift of prophecy"; but he is not named here because the intention was to show God's goodness to Abraham in his sons and grandsons; and so only one son is mentioned, and he the elder; and one grandson, and he the most famous.

Second, In answering Abraham's prayer, the Almighty may be presumed to have shed abroad the gift of prophecy among all his children: why, then, did this gift prevail in the line of Isaac and not in that of Ishmael? We reply, that God hath divided time from the day of Abraham to the Resurrection, in respect of all mankind, into two halves. During the first half was the rise of prophecy,—prophet following prophet in great numbers during this period. Then, in the second half, arose from the other son (*i.e.* Ishmael) a single prophet, who combined in his person all the attributes that were in the former race, and whose mission was for all mankind, namely, Mohammed, whom the Lord made the last of the prophets. And so the world remained under the religion of the seed of Isaac during the first cycle for above 4000 years, and it shall equally remain under the faith of the seed of Ishmael during a like cycle. —*Râzi.*

Remarks.— The attentive reader will not fail to observe that the Imâm here changes his front, and gives quite another reason for the omission of Ishmael's name. Formerly he told us it was omitted, the object being to mention Isaac as the progenitor of the race of Israelitish prophets. Here he tells us that Ishmael, though one of the gifts of God to Abraham, is not mentioned, since Isaac being the first-born, it was natural only to name him as the representative of the family;—a strange slip, seeing that Ishmael was born long before Isaac who was the son of Abraham's old age. And supposing that Ishmael, the ancestor (as the Imâm has it) of the Prince of the Prophets, was thus given as a blessing to Abraham, it would surely have been all the more incumbent that, as the first-born, he should here have been named. No; the real reason why he is not named was (as Beidhawi says), that Isaac and Jacob were "the root" and ancestry of the race of the prophets, and that from them was to spring Him in whom "all the nations of the earth would be blessed";[1]—further, because Isaac was the child of promise (as we see both in the Tourât and Coran), according to the angelic message to Abraham and Sarah, whereas Ishmael was born of the bondsmaid Hagar, without promise or heavenly message. Again, the promise of the gift of prophecy

[1] Gen. xxii. 18, xxvi. 4, xxviii. 14.

to the seed of Abraham, in immediate connection with the notice of Isaac and Jacob as progeny given by covenant to Abraham, is in strong contrast with the absence of any such promise in passages where Ishmael is named.[1]

And where did the Imâm learn that the Almighty divided the ages into two cycles, assigning the first of 4000 years to the prophets of the Beni Israel, and the second of a like period as the era of Mohammed over all mankind, etc.? Altogether opposed to fact! For the religion of Jesus, *i.e.* of the Beni Israel, is still predominant; spread over the whole earth,—its followers some three times the number of the followers of Mohammed, and vastly exceeding in name and authority all the other religions in the world.

Again, how can the Imâm say that in Mohammed were centred all the graces of the prophets of Israel? We need notice but two of these. As for Moses, the Lord spake with him face to face, and gave to him the Tables of the Law, on Mount Horeb, before assembled Israel; and his signs and miracles are known to all. But, as for Mohammed, the Almighty (as you hold) did not speak with him directly at all, but sent Gabriel with His messages; and as for miracles, he showed none, as we have seen in the first chapter. Where, then, are the graces of Moses to be found in Mohammed? And then, as to Jesus Christ, how vastly His dignity exceeds even that of Moses! Born without an earthly father, He is called

---

[1] Compare also Sura Al Anbia (xxi.) v. 82; and Sura ﺺ (xxxviii.) v. 46.

in the Coran "the Spirit of God and His Word";
neither was there any fault found in Him, or need
of forgiveness, the Coran itself being witness; while
His miracles surpassed those of Moses, in that (as the
Coran says) He raised the dead, healed the blind and
the leper, and made living creatures out of clay. Of
Mohammed, on the other hand, none of such wonderful things can be said, either in respect of birth or
works; and that he needed forgiveness is plain from
the text: "Verily WE have forgiven thee the sins
that have gone before and those that follow after."
How different from the pure and holy Jesus, gentle,
compassionate, and mild, who whithersoever He
went, scattered gifts and blessings amongst the poor
and wretched! Where, then, is the comparison of
Mohammed with the Christ?

And so, we see, it is easy to make assertions, a
different thing to prove them; easy to rush into the
battle, and there find oneself all unprepared. The
Imâm could hardly have considered how unreal was
such an argument, or with what ease it could be cast
aside by the People of the Book, to have adventured
on it. I scarcely think that such weak and groundless
reasoning will approve itself to the fair and intelligent
Moslems of the present day.

V. *And WE bestowed on him Isaac and Jacob as an
additional gift; and WE made all of them righteous
persons; WE made them also leaders, that they might
guide others by OUR command. And WE inspired them
to do good works, the observance of prayer, and the*

giving of alms; and they served Us.—SURA AL ANBIA (xxi.) vv. 69, 70.

Commentary. — When Abraham prayed, "O God, bestow on me a righteous son," the Lord answered his prayer, and gave him Isaac, and Jacob also as an "additional gift"; and all were made prophets and messengers, doing His will, virtuous and holy. "And they served Me"; that is, as God fulfilled His promise, so they fulfilled their part in obedience and worship.—*Râzi.*

Beidhawi is much to the same effect; but I add what he says on the preceding text (No. IV.); Isaac and Jacob were "given," the latter as an "additional" (نافلة) child, when Abraham despaired of progeny on account of his age; and on that account Ishmael is not named. "Scriptures," he also says, mean the "Four Books."[1]

Remarks.—Thus we have four texts from different parts of the Coran, each excelling that which precedes it in the grandeur of the blessings bestowed on Abraham and his two sons. (1) WE guided them aright; (2) WE made them all prophets; (3) WE committed to their progeny the gift of prophecy and the Scriptures; (4) and all of them WE made righteous,—implying a continuous grace in close accordance with the Tourât, that "in their seed shall all nations of the earth be blessed." Surely, then, if Ishmael had been a partaker with Isaac in the promised blessing, his name would have appeared somewhere in connection with it.

On the *first* of the series (No. ii.), the Imâm remarks that the word WE "gave," signifies that Isaac was born "from the loins of Abraham, and after him Jacob from Isaac." It reads as if there was no other son from his loins but Isaac, while we know that Ishmael was also from his loins; and yet he is not

[1] The Tourât, Psalms, Gospel, and Coran.

named as coming within this "gift" from God, but only his son Isaac and grandson Jacob. The only explanation is, that the "righteous seed" in which the blessing lay was that of Isaac and Jacob, apart from Ishmael. And all this is in accord with the Tourât; for when Sarah cast out her maid Hagar with the boy Ishmael, it was told Abraham: "In all that Sarah hath said unto thee, hearken unto her voice; for in Isaac shall thy seed be called" (Gen. xxi. 12).

Referring now to the *second* text (No. iii.), I praise Râzi for his honest admission that Ishmael had no part in the promise there recited, either for himself or for his descendant,—"the last and greatest of the Prophets"; for he is nowhere mentioned as being with Abraham, or even as his son. Jelalein also speaks of his two sons being given "to dwell" with Abraham, and as being Prophets. But, Jelaluddeen! was there no other son? and why is he not mentioned as dwelling with his father? You have done well thus to drop the verse. So also Beidhawi is sound in the remark that Isaac and Jacob are named, being the "tree or root" of the prophetic race; but he adds "perhaps," because no doubt this would exclude Ishmael, who, if ancestor of the greatest and last of all the prophets, should have had the highest claim to be named with the other two, and yet is altogether ignored.

Our Author then proceeds at considerable length to review the Commentaries on the *third* and *fourth* verses (iv. and v.),—drawing from them the same conclusion that Ishmael is not alluded to as the progenitor from whom any prophetical race was to arise; that he must therefore be held excluded from the promise given to the patriarch; and that not being mentioned as one of the "righteous" progeny, is significant that there was nothing good in him,—the reason probably why Abraham prayed for a better seed. Beidhawi is also taken to task for including the Coran in "the Book," for the Book means the prophetical writings of the Beni Israel; and that expression is throughout the Coran limited to the Tourât and the Gospel, as, *e.g.*, in the phrase, "the People of the Book."

The passage ends with these conclusions: *First*, Prophecy and "the Book" are the peculiar inheritance of the Beni Israel. *Second*, Ishmael, son of the bondsmaid, was not bestowed on Abraham, like Isaac and Jacob, as "the gift of God"; nor was he a prophet, or the progenitor of a prophet. The Coran is thus in these conclusions in entire accord with the words of the Tourât, that "in Isaac shall thy seed be called"; and with the promise to Abraham, that "in thy seed shall all nations of the earth be blessed." How true, then, the words of the Coran (No. i.), "Verily, I have preferred you (the children of Israel) above all the nations"![1]

VI. *And (Abraham) said, Verily, I am going to my Lord who will direct me: O Lord, grant unto me a righteous (issue). Whereupon WE gave him the*

[1] The English reader will wonder at the space and pains with which our Author has returned with much reiteration to this argument; but he has done well to bring it prominently forward, since the doctrine that Mohammed came from the promised seed of Ishmael is one on which Moslem apologists set much store.

promise of a meek youth. And when he had grown up to be a helper to him, Abraham said, O my son, Verily, I saw in a dream that I should offer thee in sacrifice; consider therefore what thou seest fit to be done. He said, O my father, do as thou art commanded; thou shalt find me, if God please, one of the resigned. So when they had submitted themselves (to the divine command), and Abraham had laid his son prostrate on his face, WE cried unto him, O Abraham, verily thou hast verified the vision: thus do WE reward the good. Truly this was a manifest trial. And WE ransomed him with a noble victim. And WE left for him (this blessing) by the latest posterity:—PEACE BE ON ABRAHAM! Thus do WE reward the righteous, for he was one of OUR faithful servants. And WE gave him the good tidings of the promise of Isaac, a righteous prophet; and WE blessed him and Isaac. And of their offspring there were righteous doers, and others that manifestly injured their own souls.—SURA AL SAFFÁT (XXXVII.) vv. 95–109.

Commentary (in brief).—When Abraham departed from his native land to Syria, he begged for a righteous offspring, and Isaac was granted to him,—a "patient" son; and who more patient than one that gave himself up to be offered in sacrifice? As to the son offered, there is variety of opinion. That it was Isaac was held by the chief Companions—Omar, Aly, Abbas, Ibn Masud, Kab the Jew, and eight others. In favour of Ishmael is the younger generation, as the sons of Abbas and Omar, etc. There is also the tradition that Mohammed called himself "Son of the two victims," meaning thereby Ishmael and his father Abdallah, who was saved from sacrifice by the ransom of one hundred camels.[1] Al Asmai gives us this story: "I asked Abu

[1] *Life of Mahomet*, p. xcix.

Amr ibn al Ala which it was, Isaac or Ishmael; 'O witless!' he answered, 'knowest thou not that Isaac never was at Mecca; but Ishmael lived there, and aided by his father built the holy house and place of sacrifice.' There are also many accounts of the ram's horn being hung up in the Kaaba. The sacrifice was therefore certainly that of Ishmael at Mecca; whereas if it had been Isaac, the place of sacrifice would have been in Syria."[1]

Others, again, hold that it was Isaac; for the passage opens with mention of the son promised to Abraham on his departure for Syria, who could have been none other than he. Then there is mention of his growing up, and of the offering up of the same son. And so, after the account of the sacrifice, the passage ends with notice of that same son again, as a righteous prophet;—the blessing being awarded for his steadfast faith and patience in the sacrifice. Thus from first to last the passage can refer to none other. A further proof is, that in the letter to Joseph are these words, "Jacob, the Israel of God, son of Isaac the sacrifice, son of Abraham the friend of God." But, after all, what can we say but, "The Lord knoweth"? Those who say it was Ishmael, place the sacrifice at Mina; those who say Isaac, in Syria and Jerusalem; but God alone knoweth.—*Râzi.*

Remarks.—It is marvellous that with such interpretations before them the Moslems of the present day should hold that it was Ishmael, and not Isaac, who was offered for sacrifice. In the first place, we have seen that the only son promised to Abraham was Isaac, and here it was the same that was taken for sacrifice. Next, observe that this is the view of all the famous Companions, like Omar and Abbas, who, being constantly about the Prophet, must have been more likely than the next generation to have known the mind of the Prophet. It must have been the notion of the sacrifice at Mecca and Mina being more in favour of Islam, which led to Ishmael being sub-

[1] Ibn Amr ibn al Ala was one of the seven famous Coran readers, *d.* A.H. 154; and Asmai was a celebrated philologist.

stituted for Isaac; and it is impossible that if this had been the view of Mohammed himself, it should not have been known to Abbas his uncle, Aly his cousin, and Omar his confidant; in fact, if you give up the opinion of his most immediate companions on the interpretation of such a passage, you affect confidence in the Coran itself; a result the Moslem would hardly desire. There being thus no escape from Isaac, the country must have been Syria, and the place of sacrifice Jerusalem, or one of the surrounding hills, not those about Mecca. In his commentary on the next verse (vi.) we see that Râzi mentions Isaac " for his patience at the sacrifice," and this in accord with the " Letter of Jacob to Joseph"; and yet, after this and all his admissions, is it not astonishing that the Imâm ends his comments by—"the Lord knoweth"?

Similarly the answer of Abu Amr to the "witless" Al Asmai, as to Mecca and Mina having been always the place of sacrifice, is no answer at all; for Jerusalem, as everyone knows, was the place of sacrifice from the time of David to its destruction by the Romans; and it was on one of the hills in the land of Moriah that Abraham was directed to take his son (see Gen. xxii. 1–14). Then as to the horn of the ram being suspended in the Kaaba, where is the proof? As if there were no horns in the Hejaz but that of the sacrificed ram sent as a ransom to Abraham! The Kaaba has been over and again thrown down and rebuilt, and we are to believe that this same horn has been suspended there ever since! Would any sensible

Moslem for a moment accept this horn as any proof? Moreover, the place to which Abraham was sent was a remote and uninhabited mountain, not a place with a Masjid and inhabitants about it.[1]

VII. *And remember OUR servants, Abraham and Isaac and Jacob, men strenuous and prudent. Verily, WE purified them with a perfect purification, through remembrance of the life to come. And they were in OUR sight chosen men and good. And remember Ishmael and Elisha and Dhul Kefl, all good men.—*SURA ص (xxxviii.) vv. 43–46.

Commentary.—Remember, O Mohammed, the constancy of Abraham when cast into the furnace; the patience also of Isaac at the sacrifice; and of Jacob when he lost his son, and his sight departed from him. All men of action, knowledge, and wisdom; contemplation of the future life made them forget the present; exalted in the life to come; and the Lord also granted them a good name in the present world, answering thus the prayer, "Grant to me a tongue of truth in the generations to come."

Then is added: "Remember Ishmael, Elisha, and Dhul Kefl, all good men; but these are another race from the Prophets, who bore trouble in the religion of God."—*Rázi.*

Beidhawi also praises Abraham, Isaac, and Jacob for their power in God's service, their insight in spiritual things, and excellent works.

Remarks.—This is now the fifth verse in which Ishmael is not mentioned as of the family of Abraham; a difficult point for the Moslem to explain. How is it that God bids Mohammed to remember Abraham, Isaac, and Jacob, their virtue, knowledge, and grace, and not a word of his progenitor Ishmael, who is

---
[1] The comments on this verse have been here again greatly abbreviated.

spoken of as if he "belonged to another generation," and not to Abraham at all? We see, then, how vain are the attempts of the Commentators to get over this difficulty in their explanations of these texts.

Observe, also, that Ishmael is here named along with Elisha, who lived some one thousand years after him; and that they, with Dhul Kefl, are said to have belonged to a different race from the Prophets,—as if, in fact, it had been another Ishmael altogether. But, specially, it will not escape the intelligent Believer that their Prophet is here desired to "remember" the three patriarchs, Abraham, Isaac, and Jacob, without any reference to Ishmael, who had thus no title to be associated with them;—in complete accord with the promise already quoted from the Tourât, that in their line it was that the whole earth should be blessed.

REVIEW

From the foregoing texts, and the commentaries thereon, three conclusions may be drawn. (1) The children of Israel were exalted above the rest of mankind, in that the Almighty raised from amongst them the race of Prophets and Messengers, culminating in the chiefest of them all, the Messiah, spoken of in the Coran as "the Word from God and a Spirit from Him," who came to bless the world; and to them He gave the precious Book, a Light to lighten the Gentiles; a "Guide to him who is directed thereby, and an explanation of every matter." (2) That the grand purpose and end of the Almighty for mankind was fulfilled through Abraham in the line of Isaac and Jacob, the sons of promise. (3) That the son of sacrifice was Isaac, and the place of offering Jerusalem, not Mecca. Further, we may conclude that no gift of prophecy or revelation lies in the seed of Ishmael.

And the most remarkable thing is, that all this comes from the Coran itself, Ishmael being absolutely lost sight of, and cut off from the prophetical line; and one cannot help seeing the uneasiness and trouble that consequently underlie the remarks of the Commentators in their attempted explanations.

It is true that in one passage of the Coran we find this verse, " And remember Ishmael, who was true to his promise; and he was a messenger and a prophet."[1] But in this text he is not even mentioned as a son of Abraham, or in connection with him at all, but separately, and that between Moses and Idris; nor (even if it be the same Ishmael) as a " gift of God" to Abraham, like Isaac and Jacob,—a difficult problem for the student of the Coran.

Now, from all this does it not follow that the testimony of the Coran is in entire accord with the Tourât, namely, that it is in the race of Israel the world was to be blessed, and that from this seed was to arise the Messiah, the Word of God and the Quickener of the dead,—an expression which the reader will recollect is explained by Beidhawi to mean " the Quickener of the hearts and souls of mankind," and by Râzi as " One that giveth life to the world in their religions"?

[1] Sura Maryam (xix.) v. 54.

PROPHECY BEING IN ISRAEL'S LINE

Such is the Messiah as described in the Coran; and what greater need have we than of this Quickener to revive the hearts and souls of mankind and give life to the world! One in whom, by the common consent both of Tourât and Coran, all nations are to be blessed.

CHAPTER VI

PASSAGES IN THE CORAN POINTING TO THE DIVINITY OF THE LORD JESUS CHRIST

1. *When the Angels said, O Mary, verily God giveth thee good tidings of the Word (proceeding) from Himself; his name Jesus Christ, son of Mary; exalted both in this world and in the world to come, and one of those near the throne. And he shall speak unto men in the cradle, and when he is grown up; and he shall be one of the righteous.*—SURA AL IMRAN (iii.) vv. 44, 45.

Commentary.—"The Word from him" *i.e.* from "the Word," *i.e.* the essence of the Word, as one would say of a brave or generous man: "the essence of bravery" or "generosity itself." Then follow traditions on "the Messiah," so called as kept clear from the taint of sin; as anointed with oil like the Prophets, or at his birth; or touched by the wing of Gabriel when born to avert the tact of Satan. "Exalted in this world" by the prophetic rank and wonderful miracles, and vindication from the accusations of the Jews; and "in the world to come," in virtue of his exalted place with God, and intercession for his people and his heavenly graces. "The Word from him"; the pronoun "him" refers back to "the Word"; just as the same pronoun in "*his* name" refers to the Messiah. Why, then, is the pronoun not of the same gender (feminine) as "the Word"? Because the person referred to is masculine.—*Râzi.*

Beidhawi: "The angels"; *i.e.* Gabriel. The rest pretty much as above.

Remarks.—The intelligent reader will not fail to observe that the Imâm's interpretation as to the masculine pronoun (in the phrase, "the Word from him") referring to the feminine noun "the Word,"[1] —is inadmissible. For, first, it is a mere conceit of his, opposed to all grammatical usage; and even if otherwise admissible, it would make no sense; for as Jesus is "the Word," it would signify that the "Word" was from the "Word," *i.e.* Jesus, as it were the father of Jesus; whereas, the message borne by Gabriel being from God to Mary, that the son she was to bear was "the Word from Him," plainly signifies the Fatherhood of God in a way glorious and far removed beyond the fatherhood of man to son; so that in the text there is a distinct intimation of the grand mystery of the incarnation, entirely different from the crude and unnatural construction of the Imâm. Again, his remark as to the different gender of the pronoun carries no weight; for even had it been feminine, it would (as he says) have referred to "the Word" (كلمة), which signifies a Person; the good tidings would thus have been of a Person to be born of Mary, of the nature of that Person,—a manifest solecism. The pronoun must therefore refer back to the speaker himself, *i.e.* to God. And since the *Kalimat* or Word was to be of a nature thus proceeding from God, what, I would ask, must that nature be?

---

[1] "The Word from himself" (Kalimat min hu); the pronoun "*hu*" or "him" (masculine) means, according to the Imâm, the Word (Kalimat) feminine; whereas the only legitimate construction is "from Himself," *i.e.* from God.

I know, indeed, that there are too many Mussulmans who will not even enter on an argument in this matter, but simply shut their eyes and ears to it without further thought. But I trust that the *unprejudiced* and *thoughtful* reader will not let the question pass till he has considered it from every point of view, and compared it with what is said in the Gospel. It is no part of wisdom to be satisfied with far-fetched interpretations, like that of the Imám, who does not look at the text for simple explanation, but as one anxious only to avoid the difficulty involved in the simple and natural explanation. He just interprets the verse so as to square with his creed, without a thought as to the interpretation being opposed to the obvious construction, namely, that God sent good tidings to Mary of a Son, the Messiah, " the Word from Himself."

As to the name " Messiah," the Commentators, finding no explanation of it in the Coran, have wandered altogether from its meaning. Now here are two questions for the intelligent reader: (1) Why has Jesus, Son of Mary, been distinguished by this name above all prophets and apostles, to none of whom it has been given but to Him alone? (2) What is there in the person of Jesus which thus beyond all others entitles Him to the name? Who can give a satisfactory answer to either, apart from the Tourât and Gospel? Now there we find He is so called because God has anointed Him (*masaha*) with the Holy Ghost, a King over Israel and all peoples, His Son in whom is life eternal. Thus He, who in the

Coran is exalted as " the Word of God and Spirit from Him," is further distinguished by the title of " Messiah," *i.e.* anointed Prince and King over all; the first (*i.e.* the divine " Word ") being the cause of the second, and the second (the title Messiah) being descriptive of the first.

How strange, then, and unmeaning are the attempted explanations of the term " Messiah"; such as that the infant Jesus was rubbed over with oil at His birth! It was not with oil (like the kings of Israel at their consecration) that He was anointed, but with the Holy Ghost; as we read in Luke i. 35, when it was said to Mary, " The Holy Ghost shall come upon thee, and the power of the Highest shall overshadow thee; therefore also that holy thing which shall be born of thee shall be called The Son of God."

Now, turning to the reasons assigned by our Commentators for the description of the Messiah as " exalted in this life and in the world to come," we read that He was a Prince in this world because of His high prophetic rank; because His prayers were heard and answered; because He raised the dead and performed other wonderful miracles; because He was innocent of the imputations of the Jews. And in the world to come, because of the glorious place assigned in heaven to Him by the Almighty; and because of His acceptance as the Intercessor for His people: all which, coming from the pen of the Commentators, raise the Messiah far above men and angels. And truly the features of the Messiah's person, outlined thus in these two radiant verses, resemble links in a golden chain, each reflecting brilliancy on that before it, illustrating thus the sense intended. Taken all together, they manifest the marvellous nature of "the Messiah" the "Word of God"; a prophet, not as other prophets; the Anointed, not as other anointed ones; the Wonderful; unapproachable in His divine and heavenly birth; a Prince, both in this world and in that to come. Consider this!

II. *When God said, O Jesus, son of Mary! call to mind My favour towards thee, and towards thy Mother; when I strengthened thee with the Holy Spirit, so that thou shouldest speak unto men in the cradle, and when thou wast grown up; and when I taught thee the Book and Wisdom, and the Tourât and the Gospel; and thou didst create of clay, as it were the figure of a bird, and didst blow thereon, and it became a bird by My leave. And when, by My leave, thou didst heal the blind and the leper, and by My leave didst cause the dead to come forth. And when I held back the children of Israel from thee, what time thou camest to them with evident signs; and those of them that believed not said, This is nought but manifest sorcery.*—SURA AL MAIDA (v.) v. III.

Commentary.—"Ruh ul Quds": of the phrase "Holy Spirit" there are two interpretations: (1) "The Spirit" means Gabriel; "Holy" means God, as if the Lord added the term by way of being honorific. (2) Or it implies that God distinguished Jesus by the special and peculiar gift of the spirit of holiness, light, dignity, exaltation, and goodness. What he said in the cradle was, "I am the servant of God who hath given me the Book"; the very same words as he spoke when grown up. This is the singular dignity given exclusively to Jesus, such as hath been given to no prophet before him, nor to any after him.—*Râzi*.

Remarks.—Of the two meanings given to "Holy Spirit," the Imâm does not tell us which he accepts and which he disapproves, or which he considers nearest the mark,—a duty surely incumbent on the Commentator. The first is evidently wrong, as opposed to the Coran itself. For (1) the Coran never thus addresses Mohammed, though it speaks to him in such language as this: the "holy spirit hath brought (the Coran) down unto thee in truth"; and again, "The faithful spirit hath caused it to descend upon thy heart." (See Sura Al Nahal (xvi.) v. 99; and Sura Al Shora (xxvi.) vv. 189, 190.) And (2) the Messiah is elsewhere called "a Spirit from God," which the Commentators interpret to mean one of the exalted and blessed spirits of heaven, the expression "from God" being added as honorific. Now, do the words, "I strengthened thee with the Holy Spirit," in the present verse, refer to one of those exalted spirits, or to "the special and peculiar gift" of the spirit, as in the Imâm's second interpretation? The apparently inextricable difficulty for the Commentator is this: If Jesus be—as روح منه الله —one of those exalted and blessed spirits whom God distinguished as proceeding "from Himself," how could this noblest of "holy spirits" be addressed by God as "strengthened by the holy spirit": does it mean that a holy spirit is strengthened by another holy spirit? What! did the Messiah, that glorious Spirit whose place is (as we are told) near by the Almighty, need the help of any other spirit to strengthen Him for the performance of His miracles? Never! Such strengthening would only be admissible for one who was not "the Spirit of God."

This verse, with the commentary on it, is the highest possible testimony to the glory of the Messiah as far exalted above all prophets and apostles, seeing that the Almighty distinguished Him with the peculiar spirit of purity, illumination, nobility, and goodness. Now we ask the candid Moslem what was this "spirit" reserved as a special distinction for the Messiah? Is it a person and nature; or is it a gift? If you say "a gift," then what is that gift? If you say a gift such as inspiration or holiness, then I reply, that this stultifies the assertion that the Messiah was distinguished by it from all other prophets and apostles; and the expression "a Spirit from Him" would thus be meaningless. But if you reply "a Person or Nature," then it is in entire accord with the creed of the People of the Gospel, that the Messiah hath two Natures—one from God, *i.e.* divine, the other human. And only thus will you escape the maze, and find a solution of the difficulty.

III. *O People of the Book! Go not beyond just bounds in your religion, and say not regarding God aught but the truth. Verily, Jesus Christ, Son of Mary, is the Apostle of God, and His Word which He conveyed unto Mary, and a Spirit from Him. Wherefore, believe in God and in His apostles, and say not, " There are Three." Forbear this; it will be better for you. For God is One God. Far be it from Him that*

He should have a son. To Him belongeth whatsoever is in the heavens and in the earth: and God is a sufficient guardian.—SURA AL NISA (iv.) v. 128.

Commentary.—" Do not go beyond just bounds"; do not be immoderate in your exaltation of the Messiah. "The Word," *i.e.* he came forth by the word of God and His command, without other cause or any human origin. "A spirit from him": several meanings given. (1) A spirit from Gabriel's breath; "from Him," *i.e.* honorific, as you would say, "a gift from God." (2) From his being "the giver of life to the world in their religions." Or (3) being "a mercy from Him," *i.e.* sent to guide the world to the truth in their life, religious and secular. (4) There is a hidden meaning in the word, signifying that the Messiah is one of the glorious and blessed spirits; "from Him," added by way of exaltation; yet nevertheless he is but one of the prophets of God; "wherefore believe in him, as ye do in the other prophets, and make him not a god."—*Râzi.*

And *Beidhawi*: " His word conveyed into Mary"; *i.e.* caused to enter and rest in her. "A spirit from Him"; possessed of a spirit proceeding from Him, not mediately but direct, both as to origin and essence. Or "a Spirit" because he giveth life to the dead, and to the hearts of men.

So also *Jelalein*: O People of the Gospel, follow not heresy in your religion; and speak not of God other than the words of truth, free from polytheism or attributing a Son to the Almighty. "A Spirit from Him," added by way of exaltation; but he is not, as ye think, the Son of God, or divine.

Remarks.—Christians are, in the text, addressed as "People of the Book," the very name implying that (as shown in Chap. IV.) they were custodians of an authentic and authoritative Scripture. Was it not, then, incumbent on Mohammed, before assuming that they "went beyond bounds" in their faith, to have first given them the opportunity of producing their warrant from "the Book," just as we are told he gave the Jews in the case of stoning for adultery? It was surely not just to acknowledge them as "People of the Book," and bound thereby, and at the same time to blame them for holding doctrines as to the Sonship, which they could have shown him to be in that very Book. Nor is it fair and just in the Moslem of the present day, as he recites this passage, to forget the opening words, "O People of the Book," *i.e.* of the Scriptures belonging to them, its Followers and its Keepers. Neither is it just for him to hold that we Christians go beyond that which hath been revealed to us therein of the divine nature of the Messiah. It were more reasonable to say;—Bring hither the Book, and let us see whether your claim as to the Sonship and Divinity of the Christ being revealed therein, is true or false.[1]

Again, Jesus is called the "Apostle" or "Messenger" of God (Rasûl). And what more natural than that the Almighty should send His Son as His messenger, just as a king might do on any important business? Thus, over and over again, you will find

[1] Our author might here have referred to the deputation of the Beni Harith and their bishop from Najran. Mohammed held a disputation with these visitors as to the nature of the Messiah, and, when they differed, instead of appealing to their Scriptures, challenged them to curse each other as a test of the truth, and "to lay the curse of God on those who lie." The Christians, very naturally, declined. The passage is as follows: "*Verily, the analogy of Jesus is, with God, like unto the analogy of Adam. . . . And whosoever shall dispute with thee therein, after that the true knowledge hath come unto thee, SAY, Come let us call out* (the names of) *our sons and your sons, of our wives and your wives, of ourselves and yourselves, then let us curse one the other, and lay the curse of God on those that lie.*"—SURA AL IMRÂN (iii.) v. 6. (*Life of Mahomet*, p. 445.)

the Messiah called Son of God in "the Book" (Matt. xi. 27, xiv. 33; Mark i. 1; Luke i. 35; John i. 34, 49; Rev. ii. 18). And the Coran comes very near it when it names Him not only the Messiah of God, but "His Word and a Spirit from Him." How, then, can Christians be accused of "exceeding just bounds" when they call the Messiah the Son of God,—attesting thus nothing but the truth as it is revealed in the Book of which they are to this day the "People" and Custodians? A matter for reflection.

Râzi's explanation of "His Word," namely, that the Messiah appeared at God's command without intermediate cause or human origin, is surely a mere evasion. For Adam, and indeed all creatures, are formed at the command of God. Adam, like Jesus, had not an earthly father, yet no one would on that account call him "the Word from God." The miraculous birth of Jesus was because of His divine nature as "the Word," not the origin of the name. Then again, Adam, being the first of the human race, had of necessity no human father, whereas, in the case of the Messiah, His birth was a miraculous event away from the course of nature. But if the Moslem will close his eyes to the Gospel, no wonder he is misled by the untenable interpretation of Râzi.

In respect of the immaculate conception, the observations of Beidhawi and Jelalein differ entirely from Râzi. They speak of Mary as the receptacle of "the Word." Now this phrase, having been shown to signify a person or nature, the commentary of Beidhawi may at this point be interpreted in the true sense of the Gospel, viz. the descent of the heavenly nature or person into the womb of the Virgin. However this may be, the explanation entirely accords with the text, "God giveth thee (Mary) good tidings of the Word from Him, his name the Messiah." And the conclusion from this verse and the two commentaries thereon is, that "the Word," of which good tidings is here given to Mary, means a Person who existed before the "descent" (حلول), and that such, in fact, was the cause of the Messiah's birth without a father.

"A spirit from him." Râzi gives four interpretations, without telling us which is right and which wrong. In the first he says that the words may signify "the breath of Gabriel," by which the Messiah was brought into existence. God breathed into Adam, and he became a living man;[1] and here the Imâm would ascribe the same function to Gabriel. That the Messiah, who is admitted even by Râzi to be "one of the glorious spirits," exalted beyond prophets and apostles, should have been created by the breath of Gabriel,—the very idea is profane! To what inconsistencies is not the Imâm led in seeking to lower the dignity of the Messiah; wandering after far-fetched ideas, while the plain sense lies before him. There is more to be said for his second and third interpretations, namely, that Jesus is so called from His having "given life to the world in their religions"; and yet here, too, is a perversion, for it was in virtue of His divine nature as the Spirit and

---

[1] Sura Al Hejr (xv.) v. 30.

Word, that He gave spiritual life to the world, and wrought such mighty works;—not because of those mighty works that He received the title. But, apart from this, we see in the attributes given by the Commentators to the Messiah, as raising the dead, giving spiritual life to mankind, etc., a strong resemblance to His own words in the Gospel, as;—" I am come that they might have life, and that they might have it more abundantly"; and again, " I am the resurrection and the life; he that believeth in me, though he were dead, yet shall he live."[1] How close to this is the comment of Beidhawi,—that Jesus is called the Spirit emanating from God " because he was the raiser of the dead, and reviver of the human heart"! Truly, men may seek to hide the light that streams from the Son of God, but through it all gleams of the truth will still shine through. Observe, also, how remarkable is his interpretation, " the Messiah, so called, as possessed of a Spirit proceeding from the Almighty, not mediately but direct, both as to origin and essence"; what real difference between this and the teaching that " the Messiah came forth from God, and that He is the Son of God"! Strange that, after all these testimonies, this blessed Person should be held to be a mere messenger like other prophets; just as if one recognised a prince to be the king's son, with all the dignity and glory of his birth, and at the same moment stripped him of his majesty, and treated him as a common servant or mere courier of the court.

[1] John x. 10, xi. 25.

IV. *And for their saying, We have slain Jesus the Messiah, Son of Mary, the Apostle of God. Yet they slew him not, neither crucified him; but he was simulated unto them. And verily they who disagreed concerning this matter were in doubt; they had no knowledge thereof, but followed mere conjecture. They did not slay him of a certainty, but God raised him up unto Himself. And God is mighty and wise.*—SURA AL NISA (iv.) v. 155.

Commentary.—Râzi opens with a denunciation of the evils and dangers of simulation in the daily walk of life, as well as in undermining confidence in testimony, tradition, and prophecy; the conclusion being against an interpretation which would make simulation an act of the Deity.

Various explanations are then given. *First,* Many hold that when the Jews designed the death of Jesus, God raised him up to heaven; and the Jewish leaders, fearing a tumult at his escape, seized a man and crucified him, spreading the report that it was the Messiah. Now the people knew the Messiah only by name, for he mixed little with them, and so they were satisfied. And if it be asked how the story of his death has been handed down from their forefathers amongst the Christians, we answer that the tradition originated amongst a small number, who might easily have agreed to a lie.

Second, The next class represent the Almighty as causing the simulation. (1) The Jews, knowing that Jesus was in a certain house with his disciples, their leader, Yehudza, ordered one of his companions, Titâus by name, to bring out Jesus and slay him; but as he entered, God took Jesus up through the roof, and cast upon that man the likeness of Jesus; and so the people, believing him to be Jesus, took and crucified him. (2) As Jesus ascended a mountain, under charge of a guard, he was carried up to heaven; and God caused his likeness to fall on the guard, so that he was slain while crying out, "I am not Jesus." (3) The Jews sought to seize Jesus as he sat with his ten disciples, on which he said, "Which of you will purchase Paradise by taking on my likeness?" One of them agreed, so he was taken out and slain, while Jesus ascended up to heaven. (4) There was a person called a disciple of Jesus, but really a hypocrite. As this man went to the Jews to betray his Master, God cast the similitude of Jesus upon him, and he was crucified in his stead. These are the various explanations. The Lord only knoweth the true one.—*Râzi.*

The note of *Beidhawi* is to the same effect as No. (1) under the second head, namely, that Titâus was the betrayer on whom God cast the likeness of Jesus.

Remarks.—Here, again, as in the preceding verse, the majesty of Jesus above all other prophets is recognised in this, that when the Jews sought His life, He is said to have been carried up to heaven.

Next, if the reader wonders at Mohammed's denial of the crucifixion, simply in opposition to the Jews who claimed to have crucified Him, and without any reference whatever, either here or elsewhere, to the testimony and teaching of the Christians,—that wonder will cease when he remembers that Mohammed was surrounded at Medina only by Jews, and not by Christians, and that neither the Prophet nor his Companions were acquainted with the Gospel.

And here one would ask,—Did Mohammed not know that the death of Jesus at the hands of the Jews was the cardinal truth that runs through both the Tourât and the Gospel?[1] Moreover, Jesus Himself repeatedly foretold that the Jews would crucify and put Him to death, and that on the third day He would rise again; and the substance of His disciples' preaching, as we find it in the Gospel, was to the same effect, His death being the ransom for our sins. Now both the Old and New Testaments are acknowledged by the Coran to be binding

[1] Our author here quotes Isa. liii. and Dan. ix. 24-27.

on Jews and Christians,[1] how is it, then, that Mohammed denies the event which is the foundation and corner-stone of the whole? Better, surely, to have denied the Book itself, the observance of which is pressed upon them, than to have denied its main purpose. Now, may we not picture to ourselves the Christians of Mohammed's time addressing him thus, as indeed we do this day:—O Abul Casim! thou tellest us to follow the commands of God sent down to us in the Gospel that is in our hands. Good and right. Now God hath there revealed to us the history of the crucifixion and death of the Messiah at the hands of the Jews, and His rising again the third day from the dead,—all established by divers infallible proofs. Moreover, these facts, as it cannot have escaped thee, are the pivot of its teaching, that which if thou takest away, thou takest away its very heart and kernel. But if, in very deed and truth, thou dost accredit this our Scripture, now before thee, then it behoveth that thy faith be even as our faith, thyself

[1] Here our Author quotes and comments on several texts of the Coran, on the authority of the Scriptures, as follows :

"And when a Prophet came unto them from God, confirming the Scripture which was with them" (observe *with them*).—Sura Al Baer (ii.) v. 97 (*et passim*).

"HE hath sent down unto thee the Book in truth, confirming that which was revealed before it ; for HE had sent down the Tourât and the Gospel from afore, to be a guide unto mankind."
—Sura Al Imrân (iii.) v. 2.

"And WE have sent down unto thee the Book in truth, attesting the Scripture (*i.e.* Tourât and Gospel) revealed before it."—Sura Al Maida (v.) v. 49. And so, in v. 48, the Christians are urged to follow its precepts thus :—" And that the People of the Gospel may judge according to that which God hath revealed therein."

a Christian like us, and thou a preacher of the Gospel. Else thy claim, that thou dost attest this Book of ours now before thee, cannot be true; for to attest a thing, and in the same breath deny it, is an irreconcilable contradiction. Moreover, history is in accord with the Gospel narrative. How, then, can it be gainsaid?

Turning now to the explanations on our text; built on the sand, they hardly deserve criticism. For example, how could it be said that the Messiah, being little among the people, was known only by His name? We learn from the Gospel that He lived thirty years with His parents, known as the carpenter of Nazareth; travelled thereafter continually over the land of Judea, its plains and hills, its cities and villages, preaching the kingdom of God, calling men to repentance and faith, and performing miracles and works of mercy, until "His fame went throughout all Syria," so that great multitudes crowded around Him from all the country round about, bringing their lame, diseased, and lunatics to be healed by Him. Indeed, the Coran itself tells us that He healed the blind and the leper, raised the dead to life again, and brought down the "Table" from heaven. To every comer He opened His heart with divine love and grace; no wonder, then, that, as on rapid wing, they sought Him from afar, and that the eager crowds pressed in on every side around Him. And yet we are told that, being little among the people, He was known only by name!

And the view is that the story of the crucifixion has come down from former generations, started originally by but a small number, who might easily have agreed upon a fiction and a lie. So far from that, it was preached abroad from the very first, being the essence of the Gospel, as before set forth. And again, even if it did rest on tradition (as we have before seen that the authority of tradition is recognised by the Moslems themselves[1]), are we to imagine that the Apostles of Christ and His people gave forth a lie, as here supposed; these Apostles (حَوَارِيَّه) being styled in the Coran, Helpers (Ansâr) of God?[2]

Then as to the childish stories of the likeness of Jesus having been cast by God upon some other person, who was thus crucified in His stead,—apart from the criticism of Râzi against the morality of a proceeding thus ascribed to the Almighty,—the tales are simply got up by persons who see no natural escape from the dilemma. And so Râzi ends by saying, "The Lord knoweth the truth of these explanations," *i.e.* "I cannot vouch for them." Well spoken, so far, Imâm! If thou and thy forefathers had but sought for this truth, they would have found it revealed in the Gospel, "the Book" attested by the Coran of which thou art an interpreter, *i.e.* the grand truth that the death of Christ is the life of the world.

V. *When God said, O Jesus, verily I will cause thee to die, and I will raise thee up unto myself; and will deliver thee from the Unbelievers; and will make them that follow thee to be above the Unbelievers until the day of resurrection. Then unto ME shall be your*

[1] See above, pp. 82 and 134.   [2] Sura Al Imrân (iii.) v. 50.

return, and I will judge between you, concerning that wherein ye disagree.—SURA AL IMRĀN (iii.) v. 53.

Commentary.—The interpretations being very lengthy, are here much abbreviated. "Will cause thee to die"; (1) will bring thy life to an end, and not leave them to put thee to death, but cause thee to ascend to heaven; or (2) cause thee to die,—some saying that Jesus really died, but only for three hours, others for seven, and others that death took place as he ascended to heaven.

We have again a variety of views as to the simulation, some as before questioning its justice; others, that, being opposed to the universal voice of Christendom, to question it would throw suspicion on the value of traditional testimony, even on that of Islam. Others say, that if Jesus had been taken up, and a similitude not cast upon another, the ascension as a miracle would have reached the limit of compulsion.

The old explanations as to the dissembling of the disciples, their being few in number, etc., are repeated here as we have had them before, ending with the conclusion that what Mohammed here tells us in the heaven-inspired Coran, we must simply accept as the word of God, surrounded as it is with difficulties; and "it is the Lord alone that can give the true direction."—*Râzi.*

Beidhawi says: "Cause thee to die"; or rather "fulfil thy time to its end, and save thee from being slain"; or carry thee up from the earth; or raise thee upwards while asleep; or cause to die within thee all earthly desires that would hinder thee from ascending to the world above. Some, again, hold that God caused Jesus really to die for seven hours; then raised him up to the heavens, whither the Christians will follow him: "will raise thee to Myself," to the place of My glory, the habitation of My angels.

Remarks.—The text and commentaries thereon suggest three things. First, the preceding verse asserted that Christ did not die, but was taken up to heaven alive; here we are told as distinctly that God caused Him to die, and then took Him up alive to heaven,—two passages the direct contrary of each other in a divine revelation! The candid Moslem falls here into a sad dilemma; and the interpreters are fain to resort to unworthy shifts. Thus the first explanation gives an unheard-of meaning to مُتَوَفِّيكَ —namely, to "bring to a close the term of thy life"; as if the word was ever used in any other sense than that of natural death; showing to what straits they are reduced in seeking to reconcile the two verses. And so we call on the followers of the Coran either to confess the contradiction in these two verses, or to explain it.

Another instance of strange reasoning is that in which simulation is defended, on the ground that Christ's ascension without the crucifixion of one like Him, would have been wrong as a coercive miracle, "to force the Jews,"— جَحْ الْيَلْهَا (meaning apparently to force them to the faith, or it may be to give up their design of crucifying the Messiah). But, after all, what should be the object of a miracle but such as that,—for example, the quenching of the furnace to effect the deliverance of Abraham, and the miracles of Moses to make Pharaoh let the people go? How meaningless, then, is this alleged reason!

The next remark is still more indefensible. The disciples of Jesus, it is supposed, were cognisant of the facts, were aware of the simulation which took place in their presence, and told those about them that it was not Jesus, but one in His likeness that was crucified. By my life, this is the most extraordinary charge! When and where did the disciples ever say anything of the kind? On the contrary, these true and holy men wrote by the inspiration of the Holy

Ghost, and with the utmost detail the facts of the crucifixion of Jesus under the Roman government, and of His rising again from the dead and ascension to heaven;—all this the grand object of their ministry, as thou mayest see, if thou wouldest but look into the Gospel. I will only add, that simulation with the view of making the Jews believe that they had crucified the Messiah,—what else can we call it but to spread a fiction and a falsehood? and who dare suggest such a thing proceeding from the great God?

We now come to the Imám's escape from this disquieting problem. It is this:—"Upon the whole, the views we have given expression to land us in the midst of doubtful and perplexing questions; but when we remember that the inspiration of Mohammed has been established, in all that he hath revealed to us, by an invincible miracle (meaning the Coran), the existence of such doubts and difficulties can in nowise militate against the text of the Coran. And after all, with the Lord is the true direction." The Imám, seeing that all the attempted explanations fail to remove his doubt and difficulty, and are in themselves a discredit to the Coran, simply accepts the situation, however much against his will; according to the proverb,—"Escaping the bear, he falls into the pit."

For, as already shown, the Coran is not a miracle, and what the Imám here says of these difficulties militating against its text, is not this but an additional evidence in the same direction? If, then, the Coran be not a miracle, and there is (by admission) no other miracle to prove Mohammed's inspiration, how can the Imâm fall back on that inspiration, as proved by the Coran, for a sufficient reply to the embarrassing questions and bewildering inconsistencies in these texts of the same Coran? It is, in fact, arguing in a circle. The Coran is a miracle proving Mohammed's inspiration; and, again, Mohammed's inspiration is proof against inconsistencies in the Coran. The Prophet rests on the Coran; and, again, the Coran rests on the Prophet. Surely the Imâm must have known that this was nothing of an argument. And so these difficulties (which, as the Imâm himself admits, tell against the text) remain as they stand, and taken in conjunction with the earlier chapters of this book are decisive against the authority of the Coran.[1]

REVIEW

From the Texts quoted in this chapter, and the Commentaries, we learn that Jesus was exalted above all creatures in nine respects. (1) He was born without a father; (2) He was "the Word from God," or "the Word of God";[2] (3) He was "a Spirit from God"; (4) He was called the Messiah; (5)—a Prince in this world and in the next; (6) He spake to those about Him while yet in the cradle; (7) He created the living out of that which had no life; (8) He was raised from the dead; (9) He was carried up alive into the heavens. He was called "a Spirit from God" (we are told)

---

[1] This is much abridged. Reference is made especially to Chap. I.
[2] Pp. 124 and 128.

because He proceeded (صدر) from God; and "a Spirit," because "He gave life to the dead and to the hearts of men." Also the greatness ascribed in the Coran to Him "in this life," is explained to mean His being cleared of the imputations cast upon Him by the Jews; and "in the life to come," because of His merits and high rank with the Almighty; again, "in this life," because of the acceptance of His prayers, and His wonderful miracles, such as healing the sick, the blind, and the leper; and "in the life to come," because He is the recognised Intercessor of His people. Now, my intelligent reader, do not all these distinctive epithets,—which we find either in the Coran or in the interpretations of the Commentators,—point out Jesus to be of a marvellous origin and nature, far beyond that of any prophet or apostle? And, considering it all, can you blame the Christians for believing, in accord with the words of their Scripture, that He is the Son of the living God? Now let us complete the lesson of the close similarity and accord of the Coran with the Gospel, in respect of what has gone before, by bringing the testimony of both together in the subjoined table.

CORAN AND COMMENTARIES	GOSPEL
When the angels said, O Mary, Verily God giveth thee good tidings of the Word, proceeding from Himself; his name Jesus, the Messiah, son of Mary, exalted both in this world and in the world to come, and one of those near the Throne. And he shall speak	And in the sixth month the angel Gabriel was sent from God unto a city of Galilee, named Nazareth, to a virgin espoused to a man whose name was Joseph, of the house of David; and the virgin's name was Mary. And the angel came in unto her, and said, Hail, thou

CORAN AND COMMENTARIES

unto ME in the cradle, and when he is grown up; and he shall be one of the righteous,—she said, O Lord, how shall there be a son to me, and no man hath touched me? He answered, Even so, God createth that which He pleaseth. When He decreeth a thing, He but saith unto it, Be, and it is.—SURA AL IMRÂN (iii.) vv. 44-47.

He shall give thee (Mary) good tidings of the Word from Himself.

And His Word which He conveyed into Mary.—SURA AL NISA (iv.) v. 167.

Commentary.—Conveyed into Mary, or placed in her womb. (See p. 129.)

GOSPEL

that art highly favoured, the Lord is with thee: blessed art thou among women. And when she saw him, she was troubled at his saying, and cast in her mind what manner of salutation this should be. And the angel said unto her, Fear not, Mary: for thou hast found favour with God. And, behold, thou shalt conceive in thy womb, and bring forth a son, and shalt call his name JESUS. He shall be great, and shall be called the Son of the Highest: and the Lord God shall give unto him the throne of his father David: and he shall reign over the house of Jacob for ever; and of his kingdom there shall be no end. Then said Mary unto the angel, How shall this be, seeing I know not a man? And the angel answered and said unto her, The Holy Ghost shall come upon thee, and the power of the Highest shall overshadow thee; therefore also that holy thing which shall be born of thee shall be called the Son of God.—LUKE i. 26-35.

And the Word was made flesh, and dwelt among us (and we beheld his glory, the glory as of the only begotten of the Father), full of grace and truth.—JOHN i. 14.

Concerning His Son which was made of the seed of David according to the flesh.—ROM. i. 3.

POINTING TO DIVINITY OF CHRIST

CORAN AND COMMENTARIES	GOSPEL
	And he was clothed in a vesture dipped in blood: and his name is called The Word of God.—REV. xix. 13.
And a Spirit from him.—SURA AL NISA (iv.) v. 167. *Commentary.*—And possessed of a spirit proceeding from Him. (See p. 129.)	The Father himself loveth you, because ye have loved me, and have believed that I came out from God. I came forth from the Father, and am come into the world.—JOHN xvi. 27, 28. Jesus said unto them, If God were your Father, ye would love me: for I proceeded forth and came from God. . . . Verily, verily, I say unto you, Before Abraham was, I am.—JOHN viii. 42, 58.
And it is said that he is called a Spirit, because he gave life to the dead and to the hearts (of men). (See p. 129.) He is called a Spirit, since he was the cause of the life of the world in their religions. (See p. 117.)	Jesus said unto her, I am the resurrection, and the life: he that believeth in me, though he were dead, yet shall he live: and whosoever liveth and believeth in me, shall never die. . . . And when he had thus spoken, he cried with a loud voice, Lazarus, come forth. And he that was dead came forth, etc.—JOHN xi. 25, 26, 43, 44.
A Prince in this life, and in the life to come. *Commentary.*—" In this world," because he was cleared from the imputations of the Jews here below, and because his prayers were answered, etc.	Which of you convinceth me of sin? And if I say the truth, why do ye not believe me?—JOHN viii. 46. Pilate therefore went forth again, and saith unto them, Behold, I bring him forth to you, that ye may know that I find no fault in him.—JOHN xix. 4.

CORAN AND COMMENTARIES	GOSPEL
	And Jesus lifted up his eyes, and said, Father, I thank thee that thou hast heard me; and I knew that thou hearest me always.—JOHN xi. 41, 42.
. . . And in the life to come. *Commentary.* Because he hath been the Intercessor of his true people.	Who is he that condemneth? It is Christ that died, yea rather, that is risen again, who is even at the right hand of God, who also maketh intercession for us.—ROM. viii. 34.
His name, the Christ.—SURA AL IMRAN (iii.) v. 44. Verily, Jesus the son of Mary is the Apostle of God and His Word, etc.—SURA AL NISA (iv.) v. 167.	Unto you is born this day in the city of David, a Saviour, which is Christ the Lord.—LUKE ii. 11. And Simon Peter answered and said, Thou art the Christ, the Son of the living God.—MATT. xvi. 16. God hath made that same Jesus, whom ye have crucified, both Lord and Christ.—ACTS ii. 36.
Commentary. — "His name, the Christ," said Abu Amr ibn al Ala, "the Christ the King." (See p. 124.)	Now when Jesus was born in Bethlehem of Judæa in the days of Herod the king, behold, there came wise men from the east to Jerusalem, saying, Where is he that is born King of the Jews? for we have seen his star in the east, and are come to worship him. . . . And when he had gathered all the chief priests and scribes together, he demanded of them where Christ should be born. And they said unto him, In Bethlehem of Judæa.—MATT. ii. 1-5.

Coran and Commentaries

And when thou didst create from the clay as the figure of a bird, and didst blow thereon, and it became a bird by my permission.—Sura Al Maida (viii.) p. 114.

When God said, O Jesus, I will cause thee to die, and I will raise thee up unto myself.—Sura Al Imran (iii.) v. 53.

Commentary.—It is related of Ibn Abbas and Mohammed ibn Ishac, that both explained مُتَوَفِّيكَ to mean, "I will cause thee to die." Then God raised him up, and caused him to ascend to heaven. Wahb says, "caused him to die for three hours, then raised him up to heaven." And Mohammed ibn Ishac, "caused him to die for seven hours, then God brought him to life again, and raised him up to heaven. (See p. 139.)

Gospel

As long as I am in the world, I am the light of the world. When he had thus spoken, he spat on the ground, and made clay of the spittle, and he anointed the eyes of the blind man with the clay, and said unto him, Go, wash in the pool of Siloam. . . . He went his way therefore, and came seeing.—John ix. 5-7.

And they crucified him, and parted his garments, casting lots. . . . Jesus, when he had cried again with a loud voice, yielded up the ghost.—Matt. xxvii. 35, 50.

And it was the third hour, and they crucified him. . . . Jesus cried with a loud voice, and gave up the ghost.—Mark xv. 25, 37.

And when Jesus had cried with a loud voice, he said, Father, into thy hands I commend my spirit: and having said thus, he gave up the ghost.—Luke xxiii. 46.

But when they came to Jesus, and saw that he was dead already, they brake not his legs.—John xix. 33.

The angel answered . . . I know that ye seek Jesus, which was crucified. He is not here; for he is risen, as he said.—Matt. xxviii. 5, 6.

Ye seek Jesus of Nazareth, which was crucified. He is

Coran and Commentaries	Gospel

risen: he is not here.—MARK xvi. 6.

Why seek ye the living among the dead? He is not here, but is risen.—LUKE xxiv. 5, 6.

And he led them out as far as to Bethany; and he lifted up his hands, and blessed them. And it came to pass, while he blessed them, he was parted from them, and carried up into heaven. And they worshipped him, and returned to Jerusalem with great joy.—LUKE xxiv. 50-52.

But ye shall receive power, after that the Holy Ghost is come upon you: and ye shall be witnesses unto me both in Jerusalem, and in all Judæa, and in Samaria, and unto the uttermost part of the earth. And when he had spoken these things, while they beheld, he was taken up; and a cloud received him out of their sight. And while they looked steadfastly toward heaven as he went up, behold, two men stood by them in white apparel; which also said, Ye men of Galilee, why stand ye gazing up into heaven? this same Jesus, which is taken up from you into heaven, shall so come in like manner as ye have seen him go into heaven. Then returned they unto Jerusalem from the mount called Olivet, which is from Jerusalem a sabbath day's journey.—ACTS i. 8-12.

Now, dear reader, dost thou not perceive the close agreement and wonderful harmony between the passages on either side of this table and the majesty of the Messiah rising far above the rank of prophet or apostle? The various interpretations of the Commentators may not everywhere touch the mark, but certainly they come very close to it. And the passages from the Gospel in respect of the Messiah, are they not an explanation, one might say, of the various statements in the Coran, although they were, in fact, then original? But, alas for the blinding prejudice which an ancestral faith casts between the truth and the judgment, making both sage and fool at one! There is no remedy for this evil, or way out of these crooked paths, but for a man, casting this prejudice aside, to come like a little child, newly born as it were, simple and teachable, searching after the truth by the gate that alone leads to it, and praying for guidance to enter therein from its only source.

CONCLUSION

Now, having reached the end I had in view, namely, to show the testimony which the Coran bears to the Scriptures of the inspired prophets, and the evidences it contains pointing to the mystery of the divine nature of the Messiah, I would seek to address an earnest and loving appeal to thee, my true and gentle reader,—one diligent in the Coran, constant at the Mosque, and whose supreme concern is nought but the pleasure of the Almighty. May I hope for thy forbearance,—that thou wouldest give me thine ear to hear, and a kindly regard toward that which I shall place before thee? and then let thy soul within thee be the judge. For it is not to the heedless and unwise I address myself,—those that rest in the name of their faith, led captive by the bonds of prejudice, manacled with the chain of ignorance. Not to such, but to thee, my noble and pious reader, that I submit my case for judgment and consideration.

Now thou hast seen—praised be God!—the evidence adduced in this treatise in respect of the Jewish and Christian Scriptures. They are borne testimony to throughout the Coran, as in the hands of the People of the Book, genuine and authoritative, a revelation of the will of the Most High. Further, in view of the most distinguished of your Doctors, they are pronounced (as we have seen) to be true and authentic, having been handed down by continuous succession throughout the East and the West, and thus pure from the taint of corruption or change. These learned Doctors also believe that such passages as,—*Clothe not the true in the false, and hide not the truth when ye know it;—They pervert the word from its place,* and such like; —have no reference whatever to any tampering with the text, but simply accuse the Prophet's opponents of confusing their hearers with vain and doubtful arguments; preventing the truth from reaching others; putting false interpretations instead of true; changing words, not in the text of their Scripture, but with the lip in their speech; and hiding or misrepresenting the commands of God as in the case of the Jews of Kheibar.[1] There is no alternative for you, therefore, but to accept the Tourát and the Gospel, as thus accredited by the Coran. And when they tell thee, —God forbid!—as they tell the ignorant folk, that verbal corruption has crept into these Scriptures since the time of Mohammed and the Coran,—I say at once that it is absolutely impossible, scattered as these Scriptures already were, and have ever since continued, throughout all nations, sects, and churches, speaking various languages, bitterly opposed to one another, and using the Sacred text in controversy

[1] See above, p. 89.

and in their theological writings. Such a state of things renders the charge of corruption, or of any change whatever, altogether out of the question. In the interval between Jesus and the rise of Islam, that is, for six centuries, it is admitted that there had been no tampering with, or change in, the text; is it possible, then, that such could have happened since that time? Never! Further, we have seen—the Lord guide thee!—that the authority of what is thus continuously handed down cannot be impugned; for to deny such continuity, your learned men hold, would be to impugn the evidence of the prophetic office of Mohammed or of the Messiah,—the evidence even of their very existence, or of any of the prophets.[1]

And here I would pause, and ask thee to reflect. If these Scriptures be incorrupt, genuine and pure, what is incumbent on thee as one that seeks the truth alone, but to accept what is revealed therein of Jesus the Messiah, the Son of God, and of His death in the flesh a ransom for mankind? for, surely, belief in the inspiration and authenticity of the Book must carry with it belief in all that is therein. And now I think I see thee bewildered and perplexed; on one hand, unable to deny the authenticity of "the Book," the grand object of the Tourât, the spirit of prophecy, and the doctrines of the Gospel; on the other, equally unable to reconcile all this with the teaching of Islam, and fearing to recognise anything opposed to the Coran, as calculated to lead on to disbelief in the revelation itself, and doing despite

[1] See pp. 82, 134.

thereto. The writer deeply sympathises with thee in thy struggle and distress;—so often suffered by those who reach this solemn stage of conflicting thought,—who feel as if they could not relax their hold on the belief inherited from their forefathers, which is yet opposed to what is now seen and apprehended. Yet would I fain hope that reflection upon what has been advanced in the last two chapters, with a single eye and a mind unprejudiced, may dissipate the cloud of thy bewilderment, and let thee go forth as one whose shackles are undone, in grateful liberty.

As a house must stand on a firm foundation, so Chapter V. is the foundation of Chapter VI.; let us therefore first revert to it, and may the Lord guide thee aright! Now in the Fifth chapter thou wilt find these two positions established;—namely (1) that Isaac and Jacob were the sons of promise to Abraham, and (2) that in their line was to be the gift of prophecy and of the Scriptures. Ishmael and Esau are left entirely out. The passages quoted from the Coran all point with one finger to the race of Isaac and Jacob as that in which the grand purpose of the Almighty is to be wrought out; and for this end the children of Israel are "preferred beyond all creatures,"—exalted above all the world as the channels of spiritual blessing. The Commentators, blinded by prejudice, too often miss the point; yet ever and anon, even in their interpretations, the truth appears. The Commentators have passed away; but, thank God, the texts of the Coran remain,—a witness to the grand truth, that it is in the line of Isaac and Jacob we must look for "Prophecy" and "the Book." These passages bear witness that "God left, as an inheritance to the children of Israel, the Book, a direction and an admonition to men of understanding," and that in this race the whole world is to be blessed;[1]—promises which find their full and only accomplishment in the Messiah, the Redeemer of the world, of the race of Jacob,—He of whose coming the prophets spake, and whom they magnify as a blessing to all the world,—"a Light to them that sit in darkness and in the shadow of death." Here, then, the Gospel and the Coran are at one, declaring, namely, that the Messiah came as a Blessing and Mercy to all people.

We pass on to the argument in the Sixth chapter, which might be called an immoveable bulwark, built on the foregoing as its firm foundation. It is this; that the "the Word of God" announced to Mary was a Person which existed before entering her womb; and that this Person, proceeding from God and of the Divine essence, was conceived by her, which is the cause of the Messiah being born without an earthly father. Verily the account thus set forth in the Coran of the divine origin of the Messiah, the description of Him as "the Word of God," and "a Spirit from Him," His marvellous birth, and his wonderful works, all cast a clear light on his Divinity. It is true that the interpreters of the Coran deny the Divine Nature thus proved by these signs and plainly set

---

[1] See Sura Al Mamun (xl.) v. 51, and above, p. 109.

forth in the Gospel, being led thereto by the supposition that it detracts from the Unity of the Godhead. But I would ask,—Does it consist with the independence of the soul to bind itself to the interpretation of Commentators? Is it not more fitting to use the intelligence which God has given us, in finding out for ourselves what is the most natural meaning of the text? And thou hast seen that certain of the Commentators come singularly near the true interpretation, while some are far off from it, and others again between the two. In fact, as one reads their explanations, they seem all to be hovering round one object,—and that is how best to lower the Messiah, "the Word of God and His Spirit," to the rank of other prophets and apostles; not perceiving in these texts the Divine origin and Heavenly characteristics, which to the intelligent and open mind must assign Him a place infinitely beyond that of any other prophet or apostle. Surely no sensible man could be satisfied with these interpretations in view of the wonderful nature and perfections which could not possibly be assigned to any other than to Him alone. In view of it all, my friend, is it possible to let thine eye be darkened by any earthly blind, so that thou shouldest not see, in the light which streams all through these passages of the Coran, the glory of the Son of God? Beware! for if thou doest so, thou injurest thine own soul, and dost rebel against the Almighty.

Let us now compare the passages in the Coran regarding the Messiah with the account given in the Gospel, and we shall find in them at once *corroboration* and also close *resemblance*. There is corroboration, almost to the very letter, in the account of His phenomenal birth, His wonderful works,—as raising the dead, healing the blind, the sick, and the leper,—and His lofty rank in both worlds. There is also close resemblance, as in the miraculous birth of the Messiah, and His name "the Word of God and a Spirit from Him,"—coming very near the words of the Gospel in which He is called "the Word of God" and "the Son of God"; the description in both pointing, in fact, to a nature far exalted above all creation. Indeed, the Coran, and the Moslem traditions, in some things go even beyond the Gospel;—the former telling us that Jesus spake to those about him while yet in the cradle, and made a living bird out of clay. The latter, that at the time of his birth the idols throughout the world hung down their heads; and that whereas at birth every son of Adam screams at the prick of Satan, Mary and her Son were alone free from his touch, the Almighty having caused Satan to retire humbled and disgraced when he came for the purpose ; also that a host of angels surrounded the infant, so that Satan was unable to approach.[1]

Does it, then, approve itself to thy reason, that the Almighty should have caused such marvels to surround the Messiah, and that the order of nature should have been broken at His birth without some great purpose? Impossible! And doth not thy soul search high and low to get at the secret of the mystery? Is it to be found in the Coran? Nay, my friend, it is not there.

[1] Quoted from the *Kitab Ahya* of the Imâm al Ghazaly.

True, the Coran gives thee some precious glimpses of
the Messiah's greatness; but it stops short of unveiling
His glorious perfections and divine majesty. It leads
to the portal, but fails to open the door; it kindles the
flame, but leaves it in the heart a longing and unsatis-
fied desire. Art thou, then, content that this question,
in which the highest of human interests are bound up,
remain unsolved? How now, if someone should re-
late to thee a marvellous tale leading up to a point of
intensest interest to thyself, and there stopped short,
wouldest thou be content, and not rather beg of him to
continue his story? And should he say, "I know no
more than I have told thee," wouldest thou not ask
him to tell thee from whom he learned the story, or
where he read it, and where it was to be found; and
when he told thee, wouldest thou not exhaust every
effort to get and read it for thyself, at whatever toil
or risk? Now, by my life! this is precisely what the
Coran hath done in respect of the Saviour, Christ. It
hath told thee of His wondrous nature and life, as
taken from the Gospel, but stopped short at the grand
purpose of it all, and said not one word about it. It
lifts thee, as it were, halfway out of the pit, then
leaves thee there, neither raising thee farther nor
letting thee drop. It fails to point to the Book
from which nearly all it tells thee has been taken,
namely, the Gospel, which alone can show thee the
completion of the story, and unveil the mystery of
which but half is told thee in the Coran; or send
thee to the Possessors of that Book, to whom, indeed,
Mohammed was himself referred for relief to his

soul, and settlement of the doubts arising in his heart.[1]

And now, my friend, as thou believest in the inspiration of the texts that have been quoted from the Coran, and must see that it is incumbent on thee to find out their full meaning and the lesson they would teach; seeing also—the Lord help thee!—that thou art aware of the authenticity of the Tourât and Gospel, whose end and object is the incarnate Son of God, who hath redeemed us from our sins by His own blood; seeing, further, that these verses of the Coran agree with the Tourât and Gospel to a far greater degree (as we have seen) than with the views of the Commentators,—what becomes the duty incumbent on thee? Wilt thou follow the careless worldling who fleeth away from any approach to the Christian faith, that which alone can throw transparent light on these texts regarding the Son of God; and say with him,—"God only knoweth what their meaning is"? Such a one recites these wonderful verses over and over as, day by day, he reads the Coran without thinking for a moment what their real meaning is, or whether there may not be some way of understanding them, and getting at the heart of the matter. As if the Almighty, having made a revelation to His creatures, should yet render it impossible to comprehend the same, and hinder them from discussion and search as to what its meaning is! Or rather, wilt thou not recognise the Messiah as raised in power and glory far above all mankind, seek the guidance of the

[1] See pp. 98, 99.

Almighty as thou approachest His Book, and study the same with profoundest reverence and prayer for guidance to learn the truth regarding the Person of Jesus the Christ?

Now, reflecting on the texts that bear testimony to the unrivalled One, as alone in His birth, His nature, and divine perfections, would not every thoughtful earnest man put such anxious questions to himself as these—

Who, thinkest thou, might that have been, conceived without an earthly father, and to whom at His birth Satan could find no way of approach?

Who could that have been, named in the Coran "The Word of God and a Spirit from Him"; called also in the Sunnat "The Spirit of God"? For what Being, one would ask, could be greater than the Spirit of God?

Who could that have been who, we are told, spoke to those around Him while yet in the cradle? Who, that could, as Beidhawi explains, give life to the dead and to the hearts of men (*i.e.* to their bodies and to their spirits); who other than the Almighty and the Holy Ghost? Who, that could form a thing of life out of clay, even as God formed Adam out of the dust of the ground?

Who must that have been (as we read in the Coran), free from all sin and frailty, who needed not as other men, even the best and noblest of the Prophets, to seek forgiveness? He, over whom death had no power, nor corruption; of whom one of your own authorities says that He remained dead but for three hours,¹ and another seven, and then was raised alive to heaven;² and who shall surely so come again in like manner as He went, and shall slay Dajjál the Antichrist, and destroy the hosts of Gog and Magog?³

Who must that have been who lived, unspotted by the touch of the world, a life of purity, an example to the innocent and virtuous; who did no evil; who was to all around gracious, generous, and kind; who commanded to love our enemies, to do good to them that hate us, to pray for such as despitefully use and persecute us, and to be loving and beneficent to all mankind, be they good or be they bad?

Who may this be in whom centre all such glorious perfections? Were manifestations of divine origin and heavenly perfection such as these ever seen in any of the Prophets? Not one! Is it anywise consistent with reason to hold Him a mere man? Never! What! doth God exalt Him, and wilt thou lower Him? Doth the Almighty call Him His Word and His Son (or the Coran "His Spirit"), testifying thus to the loftiness of His Being,—a Nature that gives Him the power of creating and that of "vivifying both flesh and spirit,"—and wouldest thou reduce Him to the grade of messenger and servant? What else should that be called than running counter to the revealed will of God; and what shall be the fate of him that opposeth the Almighty?

And now let me turn thy attention for a moment

---

¹ Namely, by Mohammed Ibn Ishac, and Ibn Wahab, see p. 139.
² Imâm Ghazaly, two references.
³ Tradition quoted from Muslim.

to Sura Fâteha. Look with favour upon it, and may the Lord graciously incline thy heart unto its words, which are these: *Guide us in the Right way; the Way of those on whom Thou hast been gracious, not of those against whom Thou hast been angry, nor of those who have gone astray.* First, let us search the meaning of this the opening prayer of thy Coran, and then of the Commentary thereon. Now as to its meaning: doth not the open and unprejudiced soul at once reply, that the way into which we should seek to be guided is the way of the servants of God, the Prophets and Leaders of old; of "those upon whom the Lord hath been gracious," the way of faith in the Almighty, the root and spring of all goodness and fear of the Lord? And who are they but those who have gone before as patterns of righteousness, some of them prior to Israel, as Noah, Abraham, Isaac, and Jacob; and the rest that followed to whom God gave "the Book," or as thou mightest call it الصِّرَاطًا, the "Way" of life. And all this quite in accord with that other text: *O Children of Israel, call to mind My favour wherewith I have favoured you, and have preferred you above all other creatures;*[1] "preferred," how otherwise than that He gave them the Book, and multiplied amongst them Prophets, until at the last He sent unto them the Prince of all the Prophets, the Messiah of God, His Word and His only Son,—or (as thou hast it in the Coran) "a Spirit from Him"?

And next I place before you some comments of

[1] Sura Baer (ii.) v. 44.

the Imâm al Fakhr al Râzi on the Sura: First, the *Right Way* is that which leads, he says, to earnest endeavour after the favour of the Almighty; and we are given, as an example, the practice of Noah, who used several times a day to retire into a covered spot, where each time he would pray, O Lord, guide my people aright! Second, it directs justly in our daily conduct, keeping midway in all the concerns of life from going beyond or from falling short. Third, the prayer is: Cause us, O Lord, in everything to recognise the marks of Thy divine nature and perfections. Fourth, guide us into the Way of those Thou hast been gracious unto, those of the just who have gone before and gained Paradise. And who are these but the Prophets and righteous men of old, for the blessing of God is on those who have the grace of faith? And so the end of it all is this,—Guide us into the Right path of their direction.

Such is the Imâm's instruction; and the lesson to be drawn is this, that the Prophet is here, in the Fâteha, directed to seek for guidance in the lives and faith of the former Prophets and Saints of God. And so it behoveth us to search for the nature and teaching of that same faith which was in these men of God; and where else is this set forth but in the Books of Moses, Samuel, David, Isaiah, Jeremiah, and other writers of the Old Testament, and in the Gospel? On these grounds, then, both the purport of the Sura, and the comments thereon, we conclude that the RIGHT WAY by which Mohammed and his followers are here commanded to seek for guidance, is the Sacred Scrip-

tures, the Way and the teaching of those upon whom
God hath been gracious,—the Prophets, namely, and
the Holy Men of old. All which is in entire accord
with those other texts:—*And verily WE have given
Moses guidance, and have caused the Children of Israel
to inherit the Book, a Guide and an Admonition to men
of understanding;*[1] and,—*Then WE gave unto Moses
the Book, a perfect rule for him that doeth well, a special
instruction in all things, and a Guide and a Mercy, if
perchance they might believe in the meeting with their
Lord.*[2] And here let me ask thee,—Hath that "Way,"
the way of the Prophets of old, passed into oblivion,
or is it still open for us to tread upon? Surely the
Sirât, the Way of right direction, can never pass
away; and where are we to search for it, but with the
Jews and Christians—"the People of the Book," those
to whom Mohammed was referred for the calming of
his doubts? Again, I would ask, What difference is
there between the two texts:—*SAY unto those to whom
WE have given the Book*,[3] and "Those to whom We
have given the *Right Way*"; for the "Way," as we
have seen, is but the knowledge of God, and faith in
His nature and perfections; the path that leadeth unto
Paradise; and this signifieth nothing else than "the
Book which is a Guide and Admonition (or Remem-
brancer) to men of understanding." Now, if the
Right Way, the precious "Book" which the Lord
revealed to the Prophets and Apostles of old time,
and caused the Children of Israel "to inherit," be

---

[1] Sura Al Mumin (xl.) v. 56.   [2] Sura Al Inam (vi.) v. 153.
[3] Sura Al Imran (iii.) v. 18.

still existing pure and uncontaminated (as hath been made clear to thee in the former part of this Treatise), why dost thou hold back from seeking guidance of it, —neither taking hold of the Book, nor striving to be led by its direction? O Hungry One, thou longest for bread; here it is before thee, and thou touchest it not. In darkness, thou searchest for light to guide thee; light is close by, and yet thou hidest thyself from it! Is it wisdom for a man to thus wander vainly in search of that which he yet knoweth to be in abundance about him?

REVIEW

Now, in conclusion, I would say to my valued Reader,— Thou hast seen that Mohammed showed no miracle to prove that he was the Prophet of God; and that which has been attributed to him as a miracle, namely the Coran, hath been proved to have none of the attributes of a miracle. Further, in respect of his claim to be a Messenger of the Lord; —it is declared in the Coran that he was not sent to compel men to embrace the faith, nor in any way to punish those who refused to acknowledge him; he was but a "Preacher of good tidings" and a "Warner"; with him lay the message, with God the account. But these texts were cancelled by other texts for political reasons; and we have seen in Chapter III. how this question of cancelment is fraught with inextricable confusion, and surrounded with inconsistencies which could not possibly have proceeded from the Almighty, and are indeed in some cases opposed even to common intelligence. Doth not my Moslem reader see that, judging from the quotations of Coran in the third chapter, there is no evidence to prove the prophetic mission of Mohammed? Rather, doth he not perceive that in the cancelment of his first tolerant principles, the course subsequently pursued was taken by him as the Ruler of his people?—a course dictated by rare sagacity, and adapted with unrivalled address and skill to the necessities of the day.

And lastly, in the next three chapters I trust that the strongest testimony has been brought to bear upon the authority of the Gospel from the Coran itself, and the most convincing evidence of the truth of the Christian faith as set forth in the Scriptures.

And now I trust that my reader will believe me when I say that I have been led on to writing this Treatise by no unworthy motives of prejudice and race, or desire simply for victory in the field of controversy; and that, to the utmost of my power, I have avoided any single word which might give offence.

Indeed, my object at the first was simply to search out the views of the earliest Doctors of Islam on such passages of the Coran as I had long been pondering over with wonder and with much perplexity. And when I saw that their explanations generally agreed with the plain sense and purpose of these texts, then I began collecting and arranging them, with an abstract of the Commentaries thereon and my own remarks, as thou hast seen throughout this work; so that all, whether Moslems or others, might with ease, and without time spent in painful and wearisome search, become possessed of these marvellous testimonies of the Coran to the authority of the Scriptures and the truth of the Christian faith.

And now I humbly trust that by the compilation of this treatise in the way described, I may have rendered a service to the candid, pious Moslem,— the most useful service it was in the power of one like myself to offer. I know too well that the best and most effective cordials for restoration of health are often put aside or thrown away by the ignorant, although indeed these have far greater need of them than men of wise and noble minds, who will not refuse a share of their attention to that which is placed before them —looking to what is said, not to him that saith it.

Now I pray God that He may make this little Book material of reflection to men of understanding, and the means of bringing Truth and Light and Blessing to His servants. May He guide and direct the Reader to Himself! And to His name be the praise and the glory, now and for ever, Amen!

SWEET FIRST-FRUITS. A True Tale of the Nineteenth Century, on the Truth and Virtue of the Christian Religion. Translated from the Arabic, and abridged. With an Introduction by Sir WILLIAM MUIR, K.C.S.I., etc., Author of "Life of Mahomet," "The Caliphate." Crown 8vo, 2s. 6d. cloth boards.

Sir W. MUIR says: "It is a work in many respects the most remarkable of its kind which has appeared in the present day. It is a first-fruits of what we may expect from the information now so steadily spreading among the Eastern Churches; and as such may take the highest rank in apologetic literature, being, beyond question, one of the most powerful treatises on the claims of Christianity that has ever been addressed to the Mohammedan world. It is singular, also, as a work which only a native Christian could accomplish—one who, though born and bred in the East, has cast aside the corruptions of an effete ecclesiasticism, and has embraced, in all its purity, the faith preached in the same lands eighteen centuries ago."

"This is a most interesting and curious book. The story is a romance, 'but its framework is primarily designed to give scope and opportunity for presenting to the Moslem reader the proofs of the Christian faith, the purity and genuineness of our Bible, its attestation by the Coran, and the consequent obligation on Moslems to obey its precepts.' It abounds in remarkable dialogues, in which the argument for Christianity, drawn from the testimony of the Coran to the Old and New Testaments, is acutely and impressively expressed. Both in its original text, and in this very interesting translation, it is a volume of great interest and importance at the present time."—*Glasgow Herald.*

"An interesting first-hand picture of the relations of 'Evangelical' Christianity to Mahometanism. It is the genuine Eastern conferences and discussions between Christian converts from Islam and the faithful Moslems that do this. Some of the arguments adduced by the converts are very interesting, especially the Christians' appeals to the Koran in proof of the genuineness and authority of the Old and New Testaments, and, on the other hand, the Moslems' objections to some Christian doctrines and their defence of Islam."—*Manchester Guardian.*

"The dialogues and conversation in the book have decided apologetic value, and the incidents, the confessions, the recantations, the imprisonments, and the exiles, etc., are often of thrilling interest."—*Baptist Magazine.*

"Wherever read it will excite and deepen keen interest in the subject it treats of, which, in short, is Christianity *versus* Islam. Even should the reader not care much about the apologetic of the book, he will be charmed with the beautiful language of the author as rendered by the Principal into the purest of English."—*Scottish Leader.*

"As a proof of the reformation going on all over the East, and a curious and suggestive sample of a new Christian literature beginning to exert so wide and pure an influence, we thank Sir William Muir and the Religious Tract Society for the publication of 'Sweet First-Fruits.'"—*Independent.*

"A book which is sent out with such a eulogium as the Principal of the University of Edinburgh bestows on 'Sweet First-Fruits,' is assured of a warm welcome in Scottish Evangelical circles. It is described as 'a work in many respects the most remarkable of its kind which has appeared in the present day,' and as 'being beyond question one of the most powerful treatises on the claims of Christianity that has ever been addressed to the Mahometan world.' The author of the little volume is a native Christian, 'one who, though born and bred in the East, has cast aside the corruption of an effete ecclesiasticism.' He here seeks to establish, in the form of a romance, which is thoroughly Oriental in colouring and texture, the genuineness of the Christian faith. The story is said to be largely 'founded on fact,' and is told in a dialectic form, between a party of Christian converts in Damascus and their former companions; the persecutions and trials endured by the former recalling the sufferings of the Covenanters in Scotland. Sir William Muir has written a preface in which he briefly summarises the tale, furnishes some interesting particulars as to the scholarly writer, and indicates how the work has been abridged from the original Arabic so as to bring it more in accordance with the requirements of Western ideas. Without homologating all that its kindly sponsor has to say in praise of the work, the volume may be commended to readers of like leanings and sympathies."—*Scotsman.*

London: **THE RELIGIOUS TRACT SOCIETY, 56 Paternoster Row, E.C.**

WORKS BY
SIR WILLIAM MUIR,
K.C.S.I., LL.D., D.C.L., PH.D., ETC.

THE CALIPHATE: Its Rise, Decline, and Fall.
By Sir WILLIAM MUIR, K.C.S.I., LL.D., D.C.L., PH.D., Author of "The Life of Mahomet," "Mahomet and Islam," etc. New and Revised Edition, with three Maps. Demy 8vo, 10s. 6d. cloth.

"The study of Islam, stationary as it is, is a study which Englishmen who represent, as Lord Beaconsfield used to say, a great Mussulman power, have no right to neglect, and in this study Sir William Muir must always be regarded as one of the most competent and authoritative guides."—*Times*.

"The volume does for the annals of the Caliphate something resembling what has been done by Green, in his 'Short History,' for the annals of the English people."—*Scotsman*.

"As the work of Sir William Muir, this book has a special claim to be received with respect; for he is the first English scholar that has written the history of the Caliphs from the original Arabian authorities."—*Saturday Review*.

MAHOMET AND ISLAM. A Sketch of the Prophet's Life, from original sources, and a Brief Outline of his Religion. By Sir WILLIAM MUIR, K.C.S.I., LL.D., D.C.L., formerly Lieutenant-Governor of the North-West Provinces of India. With Illustrations and a large Map of Arabia. Crown 8vo, 5s. cloth boards.

"A sketch of the prophet's life from original sources, together with a brief outline of his religion, so that the general reader is put in possession of all the salient facts of one of the most remarkable of careers. Sir William Muir gives an interesting appendix to his volume, in which he discusses the Koran and tradition, the observances and laws of Islam, and the differences between Islam and Christianity. He demonstrates the incomparable superiority of Christianity in supplying the wants of humanity, and in having love as its motive power."—*Times*.

"A *précis* of the author's larger works, but it is a *précis* done by the author, which makes all the difference."—*Saturday Review*.

PRESENT-DAY TRACTS BY
SIR WILLIAM MUIR,
K.C.S.I., ETC.

RISE AND DECLINE OF ISLAM. 4d., in paper cover.

THE LORD'S SUPPER AN ABIDING WITNESS TO THE DEATH OF CHRIST. 4d., in paper cover.

London: THE RELIGIOUS TRACT SOCIETY, 56 Paternoster Row, E.C.

www.ingramcontent.com/pod-product-compliance
Lightning Source LLC
Chambersburg PA
CBHW020312170426
43202CB00008B/575